SAFELY INTO THE HARBOR

Trusting the Captain when You Can't See the Shore

Susan T. Becker

"Lord, help!" they cried in their trouble,
and he saved them from their distress.
He calmed the storm to a whisper
and stilled the waves.
What a blessing was that stillness
as he brought them safely into harbor!

PSALM 107:28-30 NLT

CONTENTS

PREFACE

This book is both a compilation and a continuation of writings started a few years ago.

When our family first set out in itinerant ministry as Jeremiah 29:11 Ministries, I began sending out a newsletter entitled, The Hopemessenger. Included in each edition was a devotional thought I would write, aptly called, "Just a Thought."

The frequent positive feedback I received on those "thoughts" inspired me, in 2009, to begin writing The Invisible Woman blog. I have continued to add posts to that blog, somewhat sporadically, since that time.

When I began talking about writing a book, my husband Jeff suggested that I compile my blog posts into a book as a start. I was resistant, my head filled with other things that I wanted to write. Interestingly, as I attempted to outline a different book, I seemed to get stuck after about a chapter or so. My solution to getting "unstuck" was to do a little free writing, which just happened to fall into the pattern of more entries for The Invisible Woman blog. So, though I may be stubborn at times, I decided that perhaps Jeff was right, and that maybe getting this project done would be a good starting point after all.

As I have read back through the past 11+ years of blog posts, I have found so much personal encouragement! I have been reminded of the lessons the Lord has taught me over the years. I confess, in some areas, I needed a refresher course. So even if no one else is reached by this project, the personal benefit was worth the effort. It is my prayer, though, that the impact will reach beyond my own heart.

I haven't included all of the posts here, but have prayerfully considered which writings might bring some encouragement to the readers.

As I have contemplated a title for the book, I realized that a common thread over the years has been *struggle.* I cannot recall a time when there have not been questions and trials or when life has seemed easy. I sometimes wonder if I am the only person in a constant state of struggle and searching. I suspect that I am not. And in this year where every turn has brought a new challenge in our country and in our world, I have to believe that a little encouragement is something we could all use.

And so I was reminded of a passage in the Psalms that served as a theme for the children's ministry I was leading a few years ago. I stumbled onto this verse while seeking something nautical and sea-related in the Scriptures:

> *What a blessing was that stillness as he*
> *brought them safely into harbor!*
> *Psalm 107:30 NLT*

A safe harbor... a place of stillness and rest... blessing.

I pray that these pages will steer your heart toward the One who wants to give your weary soul some rest in the harbor.

Blessings.

I WILL TAKE CARE OF YOU

The Lord replied, "I will take care of you, Jeremiah."

Jeremiah 15:11a NLT

T he prophet was feeling discouraged.
    I know what that feels like, and I'll bet you do, too. You want so much for life to be different, for something - anything - to at least seem to be going right. And yet at the end of the day, you crawl into bed feeling weary and still discouraged.

Jeremiah had been the Lord's prophet to the people of Judah. For years he had been warning them of what was going to happen if they continued to rebel against God. But the people had not listened. Instead, they found other "prophets" who would tickle their ears, telling them what they wanted to hear. While Jeremiah was warning the people to turn from their rebellion, sharing with them the Lord's displeasure, these false prophets were telling the people not to worry - everything was going to be okay.

Everything was NOT going to be okay. There were going to be consequences for Judah's idolatry, and Jeremiah knew this. He had been calling the people to repentance, all the while crying out to God for mercy. This had been going on for years.

Jeremiah had poured out his heart to the people of Judah. He had shared the warnings of calamity the Lord was planning for them. Jeremiah begged them over and over to return to God. And he begged God over and over to change His mind.

For some time now, the Lord had been telling Jeremiah to stop praying for Judah. God knew that the people were not going to change. Still, Jeremiah had continued to plead with the people and to plead with the Lord on their behalf.

Now Jeremiah has reached a point of discouragement. His optimism is gone. The people aren't listening, and God is not changing His mind.

I can imagine that Jeremiah is probably feeling pretty worthless at this point. As a prophet, he probably feels like a failure. He feels that his efforts have been in vain. The people whose lives Jeremiah has been trying to save have rejected and mistreated him.

So Jeremiah finds himself in a pretty low place. And he is crying out to God again - this time for himself.

And God, as God does, came to encourage Jeremiah. His words were simple. "I will take care of you."

What a relief this must have been for Jeremiah. Though he knew his messages came from the Lord, Jeremiah must have felt very alone in this world. He did not have the benefit of an indwelling Holy Spirit to continually remind him of the Lord's watchcare over him. To hear the Lord say, "I will take care of you," must have offered Jeremiah some small peace in a very chaotic time.

In your place of discouragement, do not lose hope. Though it may seem that your work is in vain, that you are wasting time and energy, that things will never change - continue in the things that you know God has told you to do. Then rest in this word of encouragement which the Lord spoke to his prophet Jeremiah.

"I will take care of you."

RIGHT TO REMAIN SILENT

Be angry, and do not sin; ponder in your own hearts on your beds, and be silent.

Psalm 4:4 ESV

I 've enjoyed watching cop shows on TV for most of my life. From Adam-12 and Barney Miller as a small child, to T.J. Hooker, Hill Street Blues, Hawaii 5-O (original and remake), and many others, I have heard the phrase, "You have the right to remain silent..." more times than I can try to count. The point is that you are not required to incriminate yourself of wrongs you may have done. (This always seemed contrary to what I observed in the court shows on television where you swear to "tell the truth, the whole truth, and nothing but the truth.." But, whatever!

The "right to remain silent" is a foundational right of citizenship, guaranteed by our Constitution here in the US. This provision was made for our protection, and as someone whose spoken words don't always convey the intended sentiment, I can appreciate this right. And yet, though we are given the RIGHT to remain silent, the ABILITY to remain silent seems to be sorely lacking in our world today.

We are living in unusual times. Strange things are happening in our country and in our world. And, for good or for bad, in the midst of these strange times, the platforms from which people can speak opinions and ideas are virtually unlimited. With the technology of the day, information - and misinformation - travels near the speed of light (really, really fast!). And lately, it seems, much of what is being communicated is rooted in hatred and anger.

Not surprisingly, the Bible has something very pertinent to say on the subject. The Lord tells us in scripture that though we may become angry, we should remain silent. The New Living Translation puts it like this:

Don't sin by letting anger control you. Think about it overnight and remain silent.

Why is something so simple so hard to do? We can defend our positions, claim "righteous indignation," express our ideas as moral defense of the powerless, etc... We may get passionate, and feel justified in our anger. We may even actually be right! But once our anger begins to drive our actions, and particularly our speech, our indignation is no longer righteous. It is sin. No matter how hard we try to pretty it up, the root of the problem is sin.

This is not to say that it is a sin to get angry. Anger is an emotion, not an action. And emotions are not sinful. Our emotions are our automatic responses to the things that happen to us and around us. This is how God created us. He created us with the capacity to get angry, and so obviously He expects us to get angry. We should get angry about injustice in our world. We should care when people are mistreated. But when we are angry, we should keep our mouths shut. We should not let our anger lead us into sin.

Silence is not the same as apathy. Just because I am not vocal about a particular topic does not mean that I do not care. Silence gives me time to be thoughtful. The Psalmist goes as far as to say that we should think about it overnight. That certainly seems like a good rule of thumb. If there is an issue that needs to be discussed, once the anger has passed, it is much easier to think and speak rationally. I often find that by the next day, what I thought needed to be said in the moment really didn't need to be said at all.

In these days when anger and fear are running rampant, remember that silence is golden. Not every idea that comes into your head needs to come out of your mouth (or onto your social media page). It's a hard lesson, but one that I am trying to learn in these uncertain times.

Take some time to read Psalm 4 in its entirety today. I believe you will find comfort and encouragement there...

Many people say, "Who will show us better times?" (v.6a)

In peace I will lie down and sleep, for you alone, O Lord, will keep me safe. (v.8)

Settle down. Get quiet. God can be trusted. So rest well tonight.

DON'T STOP
BELIEVING

And the king said to the man of God, "Come home with me, and refresh yourself, and I will give you a reward." And the man of God said to the king, "If you give me half your house, I will not go in with you. And I will not eat bread or drink water in this place, for so was it commanded me by the word of the Lord, saying, 'You shall neither eat bread nor drink water nor return by the way that you came.'" So he went another way and did not return by the way that he came to Bethel.

1 Kings 13:7-10

The stories of the Old Testament are sometimes odd and confusing to me. I would love to have some more details to help me understand why God worked in the ways that He worked. But He chose not to give us more details. So I am left to contemplate and consider.

After reading this story in 1 Kings 13, I was confused, as I am each time I come to this story. A "man of God" came to deliver a message to Jeroboam, the king of Israel. The man delivered his message, what he said would happen happened, and he even healed the king while he was there. He refused the king's offers of sustenance and reward because he was compelled to walk in obedience to the Lord.

The Bible calls this guy "a man of God." His actions confirm this as an accurate description. The man has completed his task and is heading home in his best effort to be completely obedient to the Lord's instructions. Clearly, this is a man who heard God's voice and had some understanding of His ways.

But as he is going along the way, another man, identified in scripture as "an old prophet," tracks him down and invites the man of God to his house for dinner. The man of God relates the instructions he received from the Lord as he politely declines the old prophet's invitation. The old prophet tells the man of God that he got new instructions from the Lord, and so the man of God believes him and goes home with the prophet for dinner. During dinner, the old prophet gets an actual message from the Lord, and he rebukes the man of God for his disobedience. As the story goes on, the man of God ultimately gets killed by a lion on the way home, and the old prophet sees to his burial.

My initial reaction to this story is that it's just weird! Besides that, it seems really unfair. We get enough information from the scripture that we can know that both men would have been looked to as spiritual leaders of their day. The man of God did what God told him to do - boldly, and at great personal risk. When he had delivered his message, he started home, still carefully following the Lord's instructions. On the surface, the only mistake the man of God made was trusting a fellow spiritual leader. It just seems unfair that he has to die for this. After all, why should he doubt the old prophet? The prophet said his instructions were from God. At the end of a difficult day, the man of God was tired (the prophet found him resting under a tree), so it would seem logical that the Lord might send someone to come alongside him so he could be encouraged and refreshed. I mean, that would make sense to me.

So there must be a deeper principle at work here.

The best conclusion I can draw from this seemingly strange story is the serious nature of continuing to believe and act on what you know God has said. The man of God had a clear message from the Lord. He delivered the message. And he had clear instructions about what to do next. He obviously understood the instructions. But when he got tired, his faith wavered- just a little. When the old prophet came with a message that contradicted the instructions, the man of God did not pause to ask the Lord what he should do. He went with his feelings, and his feelings betrayed him.

Not every message that someone SAYS is from God really IS from God. Even if the person bringing the message is known to be a spokesperson for God ("a prophet"), we must measure the message against what we know God has already said. For us, this is the Bible. No matter how good or inviting a message or idea may sound, if it contradicts what God has already said, we must be true to the Word of the Lord. We must continue to believe what God has said, continue to do what God has told us to do, and not be swayed.

Interestingly, even after the old prophet lied to the man of God, *"the Lord came to the old prophet..."* (1 Kings 13:20). After the prophet delivered a false message, the Lord still used him to deliver a true message. I don't really understand this either, but that's a thought for another day.

For today, I think this story is a call to examine my ways and to be sure that I am walking in obedience to what the Lord has set before me. Whether there is pandemic, society on the verge of collapse, or simple weariness - regardless of what I may be feeling at any given moment, I must be careful to continue in what I know God has commanded. He takes obedience seriously, so I'd better do the same.

AN UNLIKELY HERO

And the woman bore a son and called his name Samson.
And the young man grew, and the Lord blessed him.

Judges 13:24

E ach year, I attempt to read through the Bible. Every time, I discover new things that I've missed before - verses that seem as though they must be brand new, for I cannot recall having read them before. And then there are stories that are just a bit odd, and that leave me with more questions than answers.

I just finished reading through Judges a few days ago, and I am once again puzzled. Much in the book of Judges seems incomplete, and, in some ways, inconsistent with my small understanding of the ways of God.

Which brings me to Samson...

As I consider once again the story of Samson, I am left scratching my head. After the Scriptures tell us in Judges 13:24 that "the Lord blessed him," the chapters that follow give us details about Samson's life. As I read about the things that Samson did and how he treated the people around him, I do not see a young man who is blessed of God and called to help his people. I see a spoiled, manipulative, arrogant, lying punk who repeatedly engages in sexual sin throughout his lifetime. In all that I read of Samson in the book of Judges, I don't find any redeeming qualities in him. In chapter 15 of Judges, God gives Samson a great victory over his enemies, and rather than giving glory to God, we see Samson pitch a fit because he's thirsty! He is not the kind of man I would have chosen to be a leader of any kind, much less the judge of a nation.

But clearly, the Lord saw Samson a bit differently. After the whining and carrying on, God split open a rock and gave Samson water (Judges 15:19). That would NOT have been my response...

As I read Samson's story, I struggle. I really do not understand. This is not a hero to emulate. He did not set a good example for the people of Israel to follow. His lifestyle was not characterized by godly living, but by blatant, habitual, unrepentant sin.

And to add to my confusion, consider what the writer of Hebrews has to say about Samson:

And what more shall I say? For time would fail me to tell of Gideon, Barak, Samson, Jephthah, of David and Samuel and the prophets— who through faith conquered kingdoms, enforced justice, obtained promises, stopped the mouths of lions, quenched the power of fire, escaped the edge of the sword, were made strong out of weakness, became mighty in war, put foreign armies to flight.
Hebrews 11:32-34

Samson is listed among the heroes of faith in Hebrews 11!

I find myself wishing that the Lord would have included a bit more information in the Bible about some of Samson's finer moments, because the stories that are there are not very complimentary. So I am left asking, "Why?" Why did God choose Samson? Why was someone like him allowed to judge Israel for twenty years? Why is Samson listed and remembered as a hero of faith when he lived such an unfaithful life?

I don't know if I have the answer to those questions, but as I have pondered the matter, I have been reminded a bit about the sovereignty of God. He can do what He wants, how He wants, and it is not required that I understand.

But, too, I am oddly encouraged. If God can take a "screw-up" like Samson and still accomplish His purposes, perhaps there is hope for a "screw-up" like me. Perhaps, the stories of Samson are there to remind me that no shortcoming of mine can stop the purposes of God.

So whatever mistake you're dwelling on today, I'd like to refer you to the life of Samson. I'd venture to guess that your mistakes pale in comparison to the escapades of the famous strong man of the Bible.

Be encouraged that you are not beyond the reach of a loving and gracious heavenly Father who is ready and willing to redeem your past and Who still has great plans for your future!

WEARY AND WEAK

"Watch and pray that you may not enter into temptation. The spirit indeed is willing, but the flesh is weak."

Matthew 26:41 ESV

J esus made this statement to Peter on the night He was betrayed. After eating the Passover meal with Christ, having been taught many important truths that they did not yet understand, the disciples had accompanied Jesus to the Mount of Olives for a time of prayer.

He warned them about the events that were about to take place, but the disciples didn't really understand. Jesus even told them what their reactions would be - that they would desert him. They all deny this, with Peter being most vocal. Confronted with the knowledge shared with him by Jesus - that Peter would deny even knowing Jesus - Peter was indignant: *Peter said to him, "Even if I must die with you, I will not deny you!" (Matthew 26:35a)*

And while we all cringe as we read Peter's words here because we know that, in fact, Peter does deny Jesus three times that night, we sometimes forget that it wasn't just Peter. Ten other men pledged their allegiance to the Lord in that very same interaction: *And all the disciples said the same. (Matthew 26:35b)*

As Jesus and the disciples arrive at the Garden of Gethsemane, He apparently leaves eight of the disciples at the entrance of the garden to sit and wait. He takes Peter, James, and John with Him as he goes deeper into the garden to pray. And Jesus makes a simple request of the three: *watch with me* (v.38). Jesus goes on just a little farther and pours His heart out to the Father in prayer. After a bit, He returns to find them sleeping, and after waking them, this time He asks them not just to watch, but to pray (v.41). And as Christ goes back to pray, the three disciples fall right back to sleep.

It had been a long day for the disciples. They had worked hard. They weren't at home, but had been traveling in ministry with Jesus. They were staying somewhere outside of town, but it was the beginning of Passover, and this was a mandatory observance for the Jews. The disciples had no comprehension that the Lamb was with them, but they knew of their religious obligation and they weren't sure how to address this when they were away from home. So they asked Jesus. He told them exactly where to go and to whom they needed to speak, and so the disciples got busy. Probably Peter, James, and John had worked all day setting up the room, finding a lamb and the ingredients for making unleavened bread, preparing and cooking the meal.

This was a hard, busy day. Having traveled for years in itinerant ministry, and even now, having an unconventional lifestyle that doesn't exactly look like having a traditional home of my own with a stocked pantry and my own kitchen and utensils - making a meal in someone else's kitchen is different. You don't know where things are. You go out and buy things in different quantities and forms than if you were home. Usually, you forget something (I do!), and you end up having to go back to the store.

It's time-consuming, complicated, hard work. By the time I've made the meal, eaten, and cleaned up (because when you're using someone else's kitchen, you can't just leave the dishes for the next morning), I'm tired.

And I can imagine that this is how Peter and the other disciples were feeling after dinner. Add to that the heavy conversation that had gone on around the table, and these guys must have been exhausted - emotionally and physically. But sometimes, there's just no rest for the weary.

Jesus wants to go for a walk. And then, he wants them to wait and watch. It's dark. It's quiet. And for perhaps the first time all day, the disciples finally have a moment to sit down and just rest.

Some people can do that. There are apparently people in the world who can sit down, be still, and stay awake. I am not one of those people! When I get still, I get sleepy. I can't really even close my eyes for prayer time at church! I seldom go to the movies because if I sit still in a dark room for more than a minute or two, there's a good chance I'm going to fall asleep. My kids used to have to wake me up when we would read stories at bedtime because I would doze off mid-sentence, and they wanted to know how the story ended. I have fallen asleep mid conversation on many occasions, much to my sweet husband's annoyance.

So I have some compassion for Peter. I don't think he was trying to ignore his friend and Lord's request. I doubt that Peter was uncaring or callous toward Jesus's distress. I just think Peter was tired.

And I think maybe that's an important lesson in this story - that we need to watch and pray, even and especially when we are tired. These are prime opportunities for the enemy to attack, and if we are not careful in our weariness, we may yield to temptation.

Our world is in a precarious time right now. Daily we are faced with challenges and struggles we feel ill-prepared to face and to handle. There is anxiety and even fear at every turn, it seems. And in that, there is a pervasive weariness that seems to be setting in.

In our weariness, let's be careful to watch and pray, lest we fall into temptation.

WHAT THE RIGHTEOUS CAN DO

The wicked are stringing their bows and fitting their arrows on the bowstrings. They shoot from the shadows at those whose hearts are right. The foundations of law and order have collapsed. What can the righteous do?" But the Lord is in his holy Temple; the Lord still rules from heaven.

Psalm 11:2-4a NLT

I f ever there was a time when Psalm 11 rang true (aside from the time of David when the psalm was written, of course), it is today. In the US in particular, we are seeing the foundations of law and order collapse. These are strange times, to say the least, and it can be easy to follow a path of anxiety and fear.

If you watch any variety of "news" at all - and I use that term loosely, because these days it is hard to discern fact from fiction - but, if you watch, read, or listen to news these days, there is little doubt that fear is driving the train. And when fear is driving, we should not expect a good outcome. We residents of the freest nation in the world have voluntarily surrendered so much of our freedom in recent days, it is hard to recognize that we are still living in the United States of America. And UNITED is definitely not the word that comes to mind when I look at what is happening in our country!

But the crisis we are facing is not actually a political one, though MUCH is wrong in the political realm. This is not a crisis of race or so-called "social justice," though the media would suggest that this is the most critical issue of our day. The crisis is not even a health crisis, contrary to the headlines that suggest that if we go about our daily lives as we have always done, we are evil, homicidal bullies. The true crisis is SPIRITUAL!

Surrounded by people who do not know Jehovah, who have not entered into relationship with His Son Jesus Christ, and who do not have the indwelling Holy Spirit to be their Comforter, is it any wonder that our world is spiraling into chaos?

I am reminded of an old Moody science video that I saw as a child and that I replay for the kids in my care regularly. In this video (I encourage you to look up "Signposts Aloft" and view the video for yourself), we see illustrated the impact of a pilot trying to navigate with only his senses to the exclusion of his instruments. The message here is on the importance of faith, and understanding that things are not always what they appear to be. In the same way that a pilot who trusts his feelings over his instruments can quickly spiral to the ground and meet a fiery demise, so a person who chooses feeling over faith is headed to a similar end.

As Christians, we are called to live by faith. We are warned in Scripture to be careful about trusting our feelings (see Jeremiah 17:9, for starters). As believers, we are at a distinct advantage in times such as exist in our day. Unlike the world around us, we have an excellent - perfect, actually - source for truth and wisdom. We do not have to walk by feelings!

But what about the people around us? What about the lost?

Well, the first question that comes to mind is, "Why are the people around us lost?" Yes, I realize they have free will, and they must make their own choice to place their faith in Jesus Christ for salvation. But do they know that? Have WE told them about Christ?

The folks around us have no choice but to walk by feelings, and so it should not surprise us that the predominant feelings that are being manifest are fear and anger. These people do not have the benefit of God's words in Psalm 23 to comfort them in the event of illness. They do not have the reassurance of Psalm 139 to remind them that they were not only known by God before conception, but their days were already numbered, and so NOTHING will take their lives until all of those numbered days are lived out. Without the "instruments" of scripture and faith in God, the world at large is spiraling toward a fiery death, and while they don't really understand what is happening, they know that they are afraid.

The fear that is driving our nation and our world is not going to suddenly go away. There truly are not good answers to the questions at hand without a foundation of faith in Jesus Christ. But with such faith, everything can change.

Instead of falling into fear and anxiety at this critical point in history, let us remember our call to love the unlovely. Is there really anyone you hate so much that you would not want them to have the opportunity to be saved?

Our government, doctors, scientists, and activists cannot solve the greatest problem facing our country and our world today. Only the church can do that. BE THE CHURCH! That is what the righteous can do. Share your faith. Live out your faith. And remember that the people around you only have their feelings to work with, unless YOU share with them a better way.

The Lord is in his holy Temple; the Lord still rules from heaven.

ANSWERED PRAYERS

One of the things I always pray for is the opportunity,
God willing, to come at last to see you.

Romans 1:10

There are days that I miss road life. And there are days when I don't! I have friends scattered across the country and around the world, and while I love the technology that lets me stay somewhat connected, I miss the face-to-face interaction. I miss sharing meals and having conversations and just being present, even if it may have just been once or twice a year that we would be together.

I think there is a lot I could learn from Paul. He, too, was a traveling minister. He didn't have the travel luxuries that I had - no bus, motorhome, truck, or airplane took him from place to place. And he didn't have the benefit of technology to communicate with the churches he visited. And yet, Paul's "archaic" communication - the letters he wrote to churches - make up some of the most frequently read and quoted verses in Scripture, and his words continue to speak to believers today. (Imagine what Paul could have done with the internet!)

Paul wrote letters to the churches he had visited. He also wrote letters to churches he wanted to visit. He didn't stick the letters in envelopes with stamps and addresses and drop them in a mailbox somewhere. Paul's letters were hand delivered. It kind of blows my mind to think about the investment that was made in time and effort for Paul's letters to be written and delivered. And the impact of that investment was incredible!

In my daily Bible reading, I have just finished the book of Acts and am starting on the Epistles now. I only got as far as the tenth verse of Romans 1 before I was struck with a fact I have overlooked for years. Paul hasn't actually met the Roman believers yet. He's heard about them. He's prayed for them. But He hasn't met them yet. He wants to meet them. He wants to have the opportunity to sit down with them, and share a meal, and have conversation, and just be present. And that is what Paul is praying for, because Paul understands that prayer is his best hope for seeing the dream realized. He wants to go to Rome, and so he prays for the opportunity to go to Rome.

Paul's prayer will eventually be answered.

What makes Romans 1:10 so significant to me is what I have just read in the book of Acts. I read about the time when Paul finally gets to go to Rome. You know how he got that opportunity? He got arrested! Paul gets arrested, people try to kill him, he spends some time in prison, and eventually, he is sent to Rome to stand trial. On the way there he takes a rough ride through a storm, gets shipwrecked, and snake-bitten. But he does ultimately make it to Rome.

We need to understand that the answers to our prayers don't always look like we thought they would. Usually, when I pray, I have an idea in my head of how I would like for my prayers to be answered. I often explain in great detail to the Lord how I think

He should do it. Not surprisingly, that's not how things actually turn out. So far, I have not been arrested or shipwrecked or snake-bitten, and I am very thankful for that!

The bottom line today is this: in that difficult circumstance you are facing in life, could it be that God is actually answering a prayer you've prayed? We can get so bogged down in the struggles that we end up missing the opportunities the Lord is placing before us. We get so busy talking and asking/begging/pleading with God that we forget to listen for His answer.

I encourage you to take a step back today. Pause in your asking long enough to listen for the answer. It is possible that the very circumstance you are asking God to deliver you from may be the path by which He will choose to answer.

This is a pattern we see throughout Scripture... Noah and his family went through a flood. Joseph was bullied, sold into slavery, and wrongfully imprisoned. The Children of Israel had to go through the wilderness before they could get to the Promised Land. The disciples had to be in a boat in a storm before they understood that Jesus could calm the storm.

In whatever storm you may find yourself today, consider what it is that you have asked God for. I invite you to look a little deeper into your circumstance to see if maybe - just maybe - you can begin to see that God is at work. Your prayers are being answered. Just remember that the answer may not look like what you expected.

WHEN YOU JUST CAN'T CATCH A BREAK

Now when Jesus heard this, he withdrew from there in a boat to a desolate place by himself. But when the crowds heard it, they followed him on foot from the towns. When he went ashore he saw a great crowd, and he had compassion on them and healed their sick.
Matthew 14:13-14

Jesus Christ needed a break. He was troubled on some level. He was God, but He was also human, and he'd just gotten word that His cousin/friend/co-laborer had been killed. He just wanted to get away for a bit, alone. He was looking for a bit of solitude... Peace... Quietness...

Sometimes you just need some time to yourself. Sometimes, though, it's like you just can't catch a break!

Jesus got in a boat BY HIMSELF to get away from people for a bit. He set His course for a "desolate place." He had specifically aimed for a location where there would NOT be people and work and requests and demands and neediness. But the people followed Him.

Sometimes, there's just no rest for the weary.

Personally, I'm not as gracious as Christ in these kinds of situations. When I'm needing a break and can't get one, I get grumpy. I may keep on going past what I perceive to be my limits, but I make it pretty obvious that I'm not happy. There may be some sighs... A frown... A rolling of the eyes... A sour expression... A tone of voice that communicates clearly that the words, "What do you need?" really mean, "I'm tired and I don't want to deal with this right now so hurry up and tell me what you want so I can send you on your way!"

But not Jesus. When Jesus needed a break and couldn't get one, the Scriptures tell us that "...*He had compassion on them...*". He didn't turn the boat around and aim for a different destination when He saw the people waiting on the shore. He didn't get out of the boat and ignore them and just walk past them. He didn't explode at them and tell them to go away because He needed a break. He had compassion on them.

He healed their sick.

But He didn't stop there. He didn't just give them a couple of minutes of His time and then continue on His way. He spent the rest of the day there with a demanding and needy crowd. When evening came and Jesus' disciples had caught up with Him, they encouraged Him to send the people away, for their own good. But Jesus did not.

The disciples, too, were probably a bit shaken by the execution of John the Baptist. They were acquainted with him and his mission, and though the disciples were not always the brightest guys, they had to have some bit of concern that the same thing could happen to them. After all, they were on a similar mission. These men probably needed some time to process the situation as well. They probably wanted to sit with Jesus and have Him tell them that they were safe, and that everything would be okay and they wanted comfort and reassurance. But Jesus put them to work.

And at this point, emotionally drained, physically tired, needing a break but getting none, Jesus proceeded to feed the multitude. He wanted to be alone, but instead He got thousands of people who were needy and unprepared and inconsiderate. And Jesus loved them. He had compassion on them. And He fed them. And when He was done, He knew His disciples were weary, so He let them off work early, while He stayed behind to finish up.

While we can look at Scripture and the nature of Christ and know that He already knew what was going to happen, and that all of these circumstances were setting the stage for the miracles of the feeding of the five thousand and the walking on the water and the calming of the waves, I think there is an important lesson for us beyond the miraculous. It is that in the seemingly never-ending grind when you feel like you can't carry on for another moment and you can't deal with one more person or one more task or one more need, that maybe, in fact, you can. And maybe, in the carrying-on beyond what you feel able, maybe your attitude need not be grumpy or begrudging. Perhaps, in Christ, we can find enough compassion to extend to others for just a few more minutes, hours, or days if necessary. Perhaps, what we have to give is greater than what we think we need.

Maybe that interruption that just came in your moment of quiet this morning is just an invitation to be conformed again into the image of Christ and to extend compassion, not frustration. That's how I'm going to try to look at it for now, anyway...

DUE SEASON

And let us not grow weary of doing good, for in
due season we will reap, if we do not give up.
Galatians 6:9

Due season. I'm not a fan of this concept. I really prefer immediate results.

Maybe you can relate.

I'm sure you would agree that life has its ups and downs. I would even venture to guess that for some of you, as for me, it feels like a lot more downs than ups. And just about the time it seems that things are starting to look up, right back down it goes. These are times of frustration. Times when it is easy to become discouraged. For me, it feels like much of the time I am simply "going through the motions."

Christian artist Matthew West has a song called "The Motions" that is all about NOT just going through the motions. I absolutely love that song, and I agree with the sentiment. I don't WANT to just go through the motions in life, and particularly in my walk with the Lord. But the reality of life is that sometimes that's all I CAN do. And in those times that all I can do is go through the motions, that is exactly what I need to do.

A while back, I found myself working in a position for which I was very poorly suited, but it was a job and it had proven effective in helping pay the bills. I was in a sales position! Crazy, huh?! I've always joked that I couldn't sell steak to a starving millionaire, and that is probably not far from the truth. But on days when I was scheduled for my sales job, I put on my "game face" and got out there and did my best to do that job. It's not like I was trying to convince people to buy a bad product or anything. As a photographer for a company that produced church directories, I made my living not just by taking good pictures, but by getting people to purchase those pictures. It was a very "people-y" kind of job, and for me that is more exhausting than a nice job making big rocks into little rocks (or something like that). So I got tired. But I kept on going through the motions, because that is just what you have to do sometimes in life.

And I guess that is really where I hope I can encourage you today. Going through the motions is not always a bad thing. Sometimes, you're "just not feeling it." That's okay. I think as a society we've forgotten that. Just because you don't feel like doing something is not always an excuse not to do it. Sometimes you need to do stuff that you don't want to do, that you don't "feel like" doing, that makes you uncomfortable or that you just don't find enjoyable. Sometimes, stuff has to be done and you just have to do it. That's real life. Sometimes, you have to just go through the motions.

In Galatians, Paul addresses the idea of "going through the motions;" He calls it "doing good." In a discussion on the subject of sowing and bearing one another's burdens, he addresses the reality that we sometimes FEEL like giving up. In chapter 6 verse 9, Paul provides us with a good reminder, which has been a source of great encouragement to me lately: *...in due season we will reap, if we do not give up.* If we will "**not grow weary of doing good**," or, in other words, if we will continue to go through the motions of doing what is good and right, Paul says, "we will reap."

In due season.

This is the hard part for us. We want to reap today. We want to see the harvest right now. And when that does not happen, we are tempted to give up. But Paul says that we should not grow weary in doing good.

And that is my encouragement to you as well as to myself today: do not grow weary.

Do not give up.

Keep on going through the motions.

Things will get better... In due season...You WILL reap, if you do not give up.

IT'S JUST A MATTER OF TIME

*Look carefully then how you walk, not as unwise
but as wise, making the best use of the
time, because the days are evil.*
Ephesians 5:15-16 ESV

My life these days feels pretty hectic. Though my kids have grown up and are on their own now, I have filled my empty nest with children. Currently, I have five - two in elementary school and three in middle school. These children have very different experiences than the children I raised from birth. Their needs are both the same and very different than the needs my own children had at the same ages. I have had to learn to navigate both the foster care system and the public school system. And about nine months ago, just as I was getting my bearings in one community and one school system, circumstances beyond my control sent me to a new community and a new school system for a couple of months before another move landed me in my current location. I have had more major "mom fails" in the past couple of months than I care to admit, leaving me feeling helpless at times, hopeless at times, and completely inadequate for the task at hand. And in the midst of all that, my list of things to do "when I have the time" just seems to get longer and longer.

I struggle. But time never seems to be on my side. Or, at least, this has been what I've told myself. But that statement is not exactly accurate.

Time is just a commodity. It does not take sides.

I have told myself, "If I just had more time, I would....", and, "Someday, when I have time, I will...".

But time is a constant. There will never be any more or less of it than what there is. I cannot manufacture more of it. No one can actually rob me of it. Each day has 24 hours - no more and no less.

My issue is not that I need more time. I have the same amount of time as every other being on the planet. And I will not have more time tomorrow than I have today. I will not have more time next week. I will not have more time next month, next year, when I retire, or ever. I have the time that I have. I may imagine that I need more time, but that is simply not reality. What I need is to use the time I have been given in the most useful way possible.

The apostle Paul encourages the believers in Ephesus to *look carefully* at how they *walk*. Walking is active - there is purpose in it. And Paul says that it should be done with consideration.

And he says to *make the best use of the time*.

Perhaps I will find more joy and less frustration in my days if I will stop "waiting until I have the time", and instead begin to actively, purposefully, and considerately use the time I have already been given, and use it wisely.

That is the truth about time - not that I need more of it, but that I make better use of the time I have. I expect that will be my challenge, "for a long time"...

GREATNESS DEFINED

At that time the disciples came to Jesus, saying, "Who is the greatest in the kingdom of heaven?" And calling to him a child, he put him in the midst of them and said, "Truly, I say to you, unless you turn and become like children, you will never enter the kingdom of heaven. Whoever humbles himself like this child is the greatest in the kingdom of heaven. "Whoever receives one such child in my name receives me, but whoever causes one of these little ones who believe in me to sin, it would be better for him to have a great millstone fastened around his neck and to be drowned in the depth of the sea.

"See that you do not despise one of these little ones. For I tell you that in heaven their angels always see the face of my Father who is in heaven.
Matthew 18:1-6,10 ESV

Most of us have a pretty messed up understanding of "greatness." When we hear the word "great" we tend to think of individuals in places of power, those with money, or people of fame. In my head, I can hear the voice from the old Wizard of Oz movie saying, "I am Oz, the great and powerful!"

"Great" is a term that speaks of awe, prestige or respect, or implies experience. Or so we tend to think...

When Jesus was asked to identify greatness, He didn't name a government leader. He did not identify a person of wealth. He didn't even point to the very religious. He brought out a child.

Our challenge as believers, as stated in Ephesians 5:1-2 is to, *"Imitate God, therefore, in everything you do, because you are his dear children. Live a life filled with love, following the example of Christ..."*

So if we are going to follow the example of Christ, we must value what He values. The Scriptures tell us that what He values is children. We must never lose sight of that important fact.

With that in mind, the magnitude of what I am called to do as a houseparent to children in the foster care system becomes a bit more clear. I have been entrusted to care for those who Jesus referred to as the "greatest in the kingdom of heaven." It is not a responsibility to be taken lightly.

In the current political climate where the work we do and the ways in which we do it are under close scrutiny from government agencies and various social service organizations, it is easy to lose sight of what really matters. On many levels, the way we are required to care for children is often dictated by people who have little comprehension of the needs of children or of "the system" within which we operate, and while we are working overtime to demonstrate to these "powers that be" that we are caring for children efficiently and effectively, we have to be careful to remember that that is not the most important thing.

What is most important is that we are caring for the sector of humanity that is special to Jesus. And not only are children important to Christ, they are the priority of God the Father. That children have their own guardian angels is more than just a sweet bedtime story platitude. It is, in fact, biblical truth. Children not only have their own "guardian angels" - their angels have the inside line to the Father. The scripture says that in heaven THEIR angels ALWAYS see the face of the Father!

This beautiful fact is at once both weighty and freeing. *The angels who watch over the children in my care are ever in the presence of the Father*, so I must walk wisely. (Talk about close scrutiny!) But on the other hand, there is no need that will ever go unnoticed. On the hard days, and the days when I am weary, or frustrated, or feeling at the end of my rope, I am not alone in this work because *the angels who watch over the children in my care are ever in the presence of the Father.* What better support system could I possibly ask for?

MAKING PEACE

*When a man's ways please the Lord, he makes
even his enemies to be at peace with him.*

Proverbs 16:7 ESV

It's been a rough season. Who am I kidding - it's always a rough season! Every season of life seems to bring its own challenges, and I have yet to go through a season of smooth sailing. I'm not saying it's not possible, but I have never experienced it.

And that's not unexpected. Jesus plainly told us, "In this world you WILL have trouble..." (John 16:33 emphasis mine). He didn't say that trouble was simply "possible". He didn't say, "you MAY have trouble." Jesus presented difficulties in life as a sure thing. So really, I shouldn't be surprised when life is hard.

"But I just wish things were different!" I've heard that a million times, and said it just as often. And maybe, that is where we can find some hope today.

I have heard (and said) that what's wrong with the world is people. As a die-hard introvert, I find that my greatest frustrations come from interactions with people. Life would be so much simpler if it just wasn't so "people-y"!

But people are everywhere! And interacting with people is unavoidable. That is not something that the introvert in me likes to acknowledge, but it is truth.

When I get frustrated with people, it is my nature to conclude that they have a problem. I clearly see what is going on, and the fact that others don't see it must be a clear indication that something is wrong with them. They must be blind or misguided or ill-intentioned or just ignorant.

And it's possible that that's what's true. Sometimes people don't act very nicely. Sometimes people are mean. Often, people are thoughtless, careless, and insensitive. And sometimes people are just plain wrong!

But that doesn't mean that we can't get along.

When there is a rift in a relationship, I tend to blame the other person. After all, I know that I am right! I may be wrong, or, in fact, I may be "right," but if there's a problem between us, I'm not right. My facts may be accurate, but if we aren't getting along, I'm definitely not right. The Scriptures are painfully clear on this point.

If you and I aren't getting along, I am to blame. I am the guilty party. You may or may not be wrong. But I am not right with God. No matter how much time I have spent in the Word, how much time I have spent talking to God in prayer, how many church services or small group studies I've attended, I am not spiritually right. If there is a problem in our relationship, it is MY responsibility.

The scripture says that, *"When a man's ways please the Lord, he makes even his enemies to be at peace with him."* The corollary to this would seem to be that if a person's enemies are not at peace with him, then his (her, my) ways are not pleasing the Lord. OUCH!

It is human nature to blame the other person for whatever problems exist in our relationships. It certainly is my nature. But the scripture today tells me that if there's a problem between us, it is a spiritual problem, and it is mine.

You may also have a spiritual problem. That does not release me from my responsibility.

So clearly I have some work to do. While I'm not aware of any enemies in my life, I am very much aware that I am not necessarily at peace with everyone around me. And it's not just because "people." It's because "ME."

Are your ways pleasing the Lord today? If you're not sure, just look at your relationships. If peace is lacking, you have your answer. And your challenge.

I know I have mine.

HE KNOWS

God saw the people of Israel -- and God knew.

Exodus 2:25(ESV)

This may be the most encouraging thing I have ever read in Scripture! "God knew." As many times as I've read through the Bible, and all of the times I've studied the Exodus... How did I miss this wonderful, simple statement?

Thoughts on this verse ran through my head for more than a month before I finally wrote them down now. Not surprisingly, the Lord knew that I was going to need to meditate on this passage and this thought a bit longer. As the Scripture says, "God knew."

God knew the challenges we were going to be facing.

God knew that our lives were suddenly going to feel very upside down.

God knew that my husband would be misjudged and treated unfairly.

God knew that my daughter would be frustrated and lonely.

God knew that I would not be going to Brazil when I had hoped.

God knew what was going to happen in our lives long before we did.

And He knows what is going to happen next.

But He's not telling.

Not yet.

I'm trying to be okay with that... Trying to be sure that's the attitude I'm presenting to others - that God's got it all under control. But really I'm angry - with the people involved, with the situation itself, with what this is doing to my family, and frankly, even with God. I prayed. This was not the answer I was believing for or for which I was praying. But it is the answer I got.

And I still believe. Beneath the emotions and the frustrations and the questions, I have no misgivings about God and His ways. His ways are not my ways. But His ways are always right.

During those many days the king of Egypt died, and the people of Israel groaned because of their slavery and cried out for help. Their cry for rescue from slavery came up to God. And God heard their groaning, and God remembered his covenant with Abraham, with Isaac, and with Jacob. God saw the people of Israel--<u>and God knew</u>.

When His people groaned and cried out in Egypt, God heard, He remembered, He saw, and He knew.

That's really all that matters in times like these. The children of Israel were in a much more desperate situation than mine. Many of you, my friends, are facing much more difficult trials than those facing me. But whatever the situation you find yourself up against, there is good news for us in God's word today:

God hears.

God remembers.

God sees.

God knows!

I pray that simple fact will encourage you today. I know it is encouraging me.

PRESENT

And he said, "My presence will go with you, and I will give you rest."
Exodus 33:14 ESV

O ne word.

Right at the start of the year, I noticed that a lot of people were talking about "One Word" as an alternative to the traditional concept of a New Year's resolution. It was a compelling idea. My Bible app even offered a three day devotional/Bible reading plan on the topic. I went through the whole process, but I didn't get "a word." I got lots of words - things that I'd like to see change, areas where I'd like to see God move, improvements I could make in my own life. But I couldn't narrow it down.

So I scrapped that idea and just moved on into the new year, plowing through my usual New Year's routines. I started working out more and trying to eat a little better... (This is not a "resolution" but it is a tradition. Since I eat pretty poorly [or very well, depending on your perspective] from Thanksgiving through Christmas, by the time New Year's rolls around I either need a new wardrobe or I need to give a little more focus to my health!) Usually I begin a new Bible reading plan at the first of the year, but as I was already in the middle of a fairly intensive personal Bible study, I elected not to add an additional reading plan on top of that right now.

But I didn't have "a word."

I had some ideas of what I wanted it to be...

"Provision" sounded good to me, because it seems like that's what I'm always asking God for.

"Abundance," because provision is "just enough" and I'm tired of struggling to get by.

"Free" came to mind, or, more specifically, "debt-free," as I really want to get out from under the burden of debt.

Rest. Trust. Create. Faith. Write. Go. Health. Home. All good options, good goals, and all a part of my thoughts on the coming year.

Interestingly, nearly a month into the new year, I got a word. I don't think it's some magical "The Word" to take me through the year, but it is a word that seems to really get at the heart of what I really need in my life. It didn't come with fanfare, but it came to my mind and brought with it a bit of clarity.

And the word is...

PRESENT

It's a word with a lot of definitions and a lot of potential applications. And it's a word I struggle with.

I have a ridiculous memory. What I mean is not that I have a really good memory. I forget the important stuff. But every detail of my mistakes and all the dumb things I've said and done... that's what I remember. Ridiculous things - silly mistakes, words mispronounced, social awkwardness that probably didn't bother anyone but me. But I can't seem to forget those things from the past. And I often let those memories dictate what I do in the present.

I'm also a dreamer. I have grand and glorious ideas of "someday..."

and "one of these days..." I've been told that I overthink things, and this is true, I'm sure. I consider all the "what ifs" and "maybes" and empathize from every direction on every topic in every situation. The result of that is that I often don't accomplish as much as I would like in the here and now. I am coming to realize that planning is only as good as the action it produces. The dreamer in me often looks at what I'm doing as temporary... just until the next thing comes along, or until a better opportunity presents itself. I use the future to console myself when things are not going as I would like for them to. I'd tell you that it's how I keep hope alive, but really it's just how I keep from committing to the present.

When Jesus taught the disciples to pray, He spoke to them about "daily bread."

Confession: I don't really like daily bread. I want tomorrow's bread today. As a matter of fact, I'd like bread for the whole week, month, and year. Then (I tell myself) I could rest in the present.

And this simple bit of faithlessness illustrates why I struggle with words like provision, abundance, free, and rest. If I can only make peace with the present, the "rest" will come.

Therefore do not be anxious about tomorrow, for tomorrow will be anxious for itself. Sufficient for the day is its own trouble. Mat-*thew 6:34 ESV*

That's the present, in a nutshell.

We live in an age when the future looks a little uncertain... Scary, even. If we expend our energy in worries over tomorrow, we will miss the blessings of today.

So that's the word for today: PRESENT.

I can't really say that's the word for the year, though, can I, since that would mean making assumptions about the future? But it's the word today. It's "daily bread."

Present.

IMPACT

Then the King will say to those on his right, 'Come, you who are blessed by my Father, inherit the kingdom prepared for you from the foundation of the world. For I was hungry and you gave me food, I was thirsty and you gave me drink, I was a stranger and you welcomed me, I was naked and you clothed me, I was sick and you visited me, I was in prison and you came to me.' Then the righteous will answer him, saying, 'Lord, when did we see you hungry and feed you, or thirsty and give you drink? And when did we see you a stranger and welcome you, or naked and clothe you? And when did we see you sick or in prison and visit you?' And the King will answer them, 'Truly, I say to you, as you did it to one of the least of these my brothers, you did it to me.'
Matthew 25:34-40

I have often heard wonderful stories from pastors and evangelists of the wonderful opportunities God gives them to witness on airplanes. My son cannot fly anywhere without making a new friend or finding an individual with a unique line of work or ministry connection to impact his mission work. I, however, introvert that I am, get on a plane, put in my earbuds, and hope nobody speaks to me!

I flew up to spend the day with my mama a couple of weeks ago, and on my return flight, I followed my normal routine: I put in my earbuds, situated my travel pillow, and put on a sermon podcast, hoping that I would fall asleep on it, as the weather wasn't great and I am not a fan of turbulence. I zoned out, but did not really go to sleep, as I listened to my old pastor sharing a bit of what God was doing in the church I used to attend. And I was struck by the impact of that church.

In 1986 as a college freshman, I had begun attending Midway Road Baptist Church in Dallas. It was a wonderful, growing little church, on the opposite side of town from my college, but I loved it there, and so I made the trek anytime I could get a ride. In February of 1987, I had a brief "spiritual crisis" of sorts, which led me to question whether I'd ever truly been saved, and I got serious with God, fully surrendering my life to Him. I moved from a burdensome false Christianity of trying to prove my worthiness to God, to acknowledging my utter UNworthiness and came to trust that what Christ had done on the cross was sufficient even for me. Free from the burdens of my self-imposed legalism, I was able to begin serving with joy every chance I got.

Fast forward a few years... My old church has changed its name and has moved twice and is apparently preparing to build a new facility in yet another location. But my pastor is still there. And all these years later, having visited a multitude of churches and having heard some of the "great" preachers, I still find myself seeking out Bro. Glenn's sermons...

And so, as I sat on the plane bumping its way through the clouds toward home, listening to a Brookhaven Church podcast, one word came to mind: IMPACT. This church where I have not been a member since 1989 continues to impact my life today. But not only that, the impact of this church around the world... well, the thought is mind-boggling! Because of the way Christ impacted my life at that little church all those years ago, I have spent a great deal of time since in full-time ministry. I have had the privilege of traveling all over this country sharing the Gospel with all kinds of people... I have traveled to Brazil and shared God's Word there... Countless people touched by the ministry of a Texas church I attended years ago! But not only those people that I've met and talked to, but also those that my children have ministered to! My son has only visited my old church maybe twice in his life, but when I see the fruit of Nate's ministry in Brazil, I see the fruit of the ministry of Brookhaven Church. And I think of the folks we've had the opportunity to minister to through the years, and those that have gone on to serve in other ministries... the young men Nate is discipling... the kids Millie has ministered to at camp... and the impact is enormous!

I'm reminded of one of my favorite Christmas movies, "It's a Wonderful Life," and of George Bailey's crisis of faith, if you will, when he questions whether his life has any meaning. I can relate to George on a lot of levels... My life, like his, hasn't gone exactly as I planned. It often seems that just when it looks like things might finally be looking up, something happens and down we go again. Like Mr. Bailey, I think that perhaps my dreams are finally coming true, and it turns out that someone else's dreams are coming true instead. But like George, we fail to realize how many lives we touch just in the process of living. It's not that we necessarily have done some huge thing, but sometimes something as simple as a kind word at the right moment, or a couple of dollars to someone in need - these little gestures had a greater impact than we ever could have known.

And so that is my encouragement to you today - consider your impact on the world around you, and remember those whose lives have impacted yours. This is how we build the Kingdom of God - not by preaching to multitudes, but by gently touching those around us.

HOPE FOR THE CLUMSY

Now to him who is able to keep you from stumbling and to present you blameless before the presence of his glory with great joy, to the only God, our Savior, through Jesus Christ our Lord, be glory, majesty, dominion, and authority, before all time and now and forever. Amen.

Jude 24-25 ESV

I am one of those special people who can trip over my own two feet, or over nothing at all; I can fall up the stairs; I can break a nail just opening a door or getting dressed. I constantly have a bruise somewhere on my body that I don't actually recall getting, but since I bump into things all the time, I am never really surprised.   Not only that, but I can even manage to choke on air on a fairly regular basis. And I literally just dropped the laptop that I'm working on!

Ironically, my name means "full of grace". I know, huh? I've always been pretty amused by that too! I'm about as "grace-challenged" as they come!

But not only am I physically clumsy, I am a social/emotional/ mental/spiritual klutz as well. I don't really enjoy social settings as I have a knack saying stupid things. In my mind, I am terribly funny, but somehow others don't always find my anecdotes all that amusing. Put me in a place where I need to make small talk, and I will leave beating myself up over the dumb and awkward things that came out of my mouth. I will have a long mental list of clever and/or witty things I could/should have said, but which will never be vocalized.

I think that's why Jude's simple closing spoke to me so profoundly this morning: *Now to him who is able to keep you from stumbling...*

Wow! I know what a big job it is to keep ME from stumbling! To think that I serve a God who is able to *keep me from stumbling*... Well, it just means that there is hope! Because He is able to *present me blameless*... My God is big enough to handle not just my physical clumsiness, but all of it! He doesn't hold against me the times I've misstepped OR the times I've misspoken! He is bigger than all that.

And the Scripture says that it gives Him **great joy**... He is able to keep me from stumbling. He is able to present me blameless. And He does so with joy! That is a truly encouraging thought for this klutz today!

Now, I'm sure you are not nearly as clumsy as I am, but I hope you will still find encouragement in Jude's words today: our God *is able to keep you from stumbling and to present you blameless before the presence of his glory with great joy...!*

THE RIGHT THING

*For I do not understand my own actions. For I do
not do what I want, but I do the very thing I hate.
Now if I do what I do not want, I agree with the law,
that it is good. So now it is no longer I who do it, but
sin that dwells within me. For I know that nothing
good dwells in me, that is, in my flesh. For I have
the desire to do what is right, but not the ability
to carry it out. For I do not do the good I want, but
the evil I do not want is what I keep on doing.*
Romans 7:15-19 ESV

This passage is me, in a nutshell. It's not always about sin, per se, but I guess that is really what it boils down to.

I was up early this morning. VERY early (for me)! I had volunteered to take my husband to the airport for an early morning flight. For once, I was going to do the "smart" thing, and take advantage of those early morning hours. It all started off so well... I stopped at Walmart on the way home (and concluded that early morning is really the best time to go to Walmart if you're like me and don't like crowds!). Returning home, it was still earlier than I normally wake up, so there was the temptation to go back to bed for a while, but I resisted. I cleaned off the kitchen table, got out my Bible study, and dug in. Motivated, I followed that up with a pretty decent cleaning of the kitchen, clearing out leftovers from the fridge, washing up the dishes, gathering all the trash from around the house and taking it out along with the recyclables, then dragging it all down to the street as it is trash day. I started the laundry, checked my email, and had some breakfast. And this is where it all started to fall apart. The early morning started to catch up with me, and I began to feel sleepy. My plan was to exercise, but then I realized that I had time for a quick nap before it would be time to take my daughter to work... Since I'd had such a productive morning already, and I HAD been up extra early, I figured, "why not?"

I knew the answer to the "why not" - that quick morning nap would be harder to wake up from than just staying up in the first place. I KNOW that napping generally leaves me feeling more tired than I am before the nap. I KNOW that exercise energizes me and leaves me feeling better. I have experienced these things over and over, and yet, almost always, if faced with the option of a nap or a workout, I will choose the nap. Ridiculous!

I vocalized all this on our drive to my daughter's place of employment this morning - after I fought my way out of my nap coma. My daughter is very kind to let me just rant on a regular basis. I don't know how much she actually listens to what I'm saying... I really hope she tunes most of it out, or she must question my sanity at times!

But as I was bemoaning my tendency to choose what make me feel bad over what makes me feel good, I was reminded that the apostle Paul had expressed a similar insanity:

For I do not understand my own actions... For I do not do the good

I want, but the evil I do not want is what I keep on doing.

Now I don't know that a nap is inherently evil, but there is a principle here that I think manifests itself in other ways in my life as well. And what it really boils down to is a lack of discipline on my part. It's learning to choose the BEST things over the GOOD things. And most certainly, always choosing what is RIGHT over what is WRONG. Or simply choosing to do what is RIGHT instead of doing NOTHING.

So whoever knows the right thing to do and fails to do it, for him it is sin. James 4:17

I'm not often tempted to do something blatantly wrong. I am the "good girl". I feel guilty if I look at the speedometer while driving and catch myself speeding. Lately, I've been struggling with the number of yellow lights I run! Lying, cheating, stealing... These are not now, nor have they ever been real temptations for me. My struggle is with doing nothing. I am great on ideas, but not-so-great on implementation.

So here's what I'm realizing: doing the right thing for me is not really a matter of doing the RIGHT thing, so much as it is a matter of DOING the right thing...

Which is what I need to get busy doing right now!

WHEN YOU'RE REALLY OUT OF SHAPE

Have nothing to do with irreverent, silly myths.
Rather train yourself for godliness; for while
bodily training is of some value, godliness is of
value in every way, as it holds promise for the
present life and also for the life to come.
1 Timothy 4:7-8 ESV

Return, O Israel, to the Lord your God, for you
have stumbled because of your iniquity.
Hosea 14:1 ESV

Confession: I have gotten out of shape. Really out of shape! Here's the thing - I knew I was out of shape, but I had no idea how badly out of shape I was. Not until I began trying to improve my condition did I realize how hard it was going to be.

Over the past few years, I have done a little physical exercise. I have occasionally gone for a "run" either on a treadmill or outside. (By run, I mean short periods of slow jogging sandwiched between longer periods of walking - not "Chariots of Fire" running!) Every now and then I have even tried to do a little strength training. Sometimes I've even worked out for several consecutive days. Because I had done a little occasional exercise, I figured I was doing "okay" - better than a lot of folks do.

But I recently decided it was time to try to put in a little more effort. I tried "running" for a few days. I noticed that I was a little slower than I used to be and got winded a little quicker, but I wasn't all that surprised. I expected to see gradual improvement, and figured I'd soon be in decent shape. Because of weather, getting out to run was becoming difficult, so I decided to pull out some old workout videos and work out at home. I tried one that I had purchased at a thrift store a while back, and it went pretty well, supporting my false sense of my actual condition. So after a couple of days, I was short on time, so I went with my old standard video I used when I just wanted to get in a quick workout... And reality slapped me in the face! I was sweating like crazy just a couple of minutes into my ten minute workout; I couldn't do even one push-up correctly; I only managed about half the expected number of repetitions on most of the exercises. It was pathetic.

Sadly, the same has been true of my spiritual condition. By going through the motions of church attendance, reading a Bible verse or two every morning, listening to Christian music, and occasionally reading a book by a Christian author, I was able to convince myself that I was doing "okay" spiritually. But as I have tried returning to some of my old spiritual "exercises," it has become clear that I have gotten very "out of shape". Things that used to be second nature - Bible study, consistent prayer, a meaningful quiet time - now require much more effort and focus. It's just not as easy as it used to be.

I am working diligently at getting into better shape - both spiritually and physically. Since I did not get out of shape overnight, I am certain that I won't get back into shape instantly.

I hope you find yourself in peak condition, but if not, there's no better day to begin a new shape-up plan than today.

RESENSITIZATION

Then Jesus shouted out again, and he gave up
his spirit. At that moment the curtain in the
Temple was torn in two, from top to bottom.
The earth shook, rocks split apart.
Matthew 27:50-51 NLT

I have been reading through the Bible chronologically this year, and this morning brought me to the account of the crucifixion of Jesus. As I read of Pilate's failure to act on what he knew to be true (He knew very well that the Jewish leaders had arrested Jesus out of envy. v.18), I felt anger and indignation that this key leader would order the flogging and allow the execution of a man he knew to be innocent.

And I continued to read Matthew's account of Jesus' death.

Then the reading guide I have been following took me to the book of Mark, where I read the same story all over again, again became frustrated with Pilate's response, but at the same time caught myself just basically skimming through the reading, as I had just read almost the identical words from Matthew.

And that is when it struck me.

While we all know the recorded details of all of Christ's suffering leading up to and including His crucifixion, what truly disturbs me today is not an ancient politician's failure to act - it is my own failure to act. How can I read the account of my Lord's torturous final hours and not be brought to tears? How can I know the truth that His death was what I deserved, and not be totally broken and humbled at the great love extended to me? I tear up when I ask for prayer for acquaintances who have cancer; I weep at the loss of people I don't even know; I cry when I read about a fictional character being mistreated in a novel; I have even shed tears at the death of a cartoon character in a Disney movie! And yet I read the true account of my Savior's life and blood poured out for me as if it is simply history? This is tragic!

And so my prayer today is that God would soften my obviously calloused heart, and heal me of the desensitization that has occurred in my life. May I never again speak of Christ's great sacrifice in such a matter-of-fact way, as though it is nothing more than the historical basis for my faith.

"God, give me a sense of brokenness and humility every time I think of the price that was paid for my disobedience to Your word. And when I speak of Your Son, may it be with the kind of passion that comes with a deep sense of gratitude at the gift I have been given. Re-sensitize me, Lord!"

OBEDIENCE

The LORD told Isaiah son of Amoz, "Take off all your clothes, including your sandals." Isaiah did as he was told and walked around naked and barefoot.
Isaiah 20:2

Have you ever done anything hard for God? When you think about "an obedient servant of the Lord," what comes to mind? I think of missionaries - those God has called to leave their homes and families to go live in a foreign country. I think of friends of mine who grew up in missionary boarding schools while their parents served the Lord in dangerous and remote areas.

Last week, I saw a car that was painted all over with Bible verses and warnings to repent and turn to God. I think there was even an extra sign attached to the roof to make room for more pronouncements. When I saw that car, I admit my reaction was to think it was probably driven by some odd, but well-intentioned person who was probably "not quite right in the head". In my mind, I just don't really think that's the most effective way to witness to people. But as I read scripture, I have to admit that what's "in my mind" is not always accurate.

As I was reading in Isaiah this morning, he's in the midst of making pronouncements on God's plans for judging the nations. He is boldly proclaiming the words God has given him of impending doom and destruction. And then God tells him to take off his clothes and sandals and walk around naked and barefoot. My first thought is that this is a very different picture of God than what most American churches are presenting. And, though I've read this passage before, still I'm thinking, "That's just crazy!" But then, I continue reading and see that not only was Isaiah's response immediate obedience - it was continual obedience. The Bible says that Isaiah walked around barefoot and naked for THREE YEARS! So then my next thought is, "WOW!" Isaiah must have had an incredible confidence in the Lord. And then I began to ask myself what I would have done...

See, when I picture an old guy (I don't know how old Isaiah was at the time, actually) walking around naked, my first thought is that he's got to be some kind of a pervert. If he's not a pervert, then he must be completely insane. But this old guy walking around naked is neither. He is OBEDIENT!

If I'm honest, I don't think I would have done it. And that concerns me. I like to think of myself as being totally committed to following God, and yet this passage points out to me that perhaps that is not true. Total commitment looks very different from modern American Christianity, I'm pretty sure. Many times through the years I have been commended for all I've "given up" to follow the Lord's leading. Sometimes, I've even whined to God about the things I've "given up". In fact, I have really not given up anything for the cause of Christ.

As I look at scripture, I find that often God called His messengers to do much more distasteful things than just walking around naked for a while. And while it is my hope that God never calls me to do something that "crazy", my prayer is that if He does, I will be obedient.

WHAT GOD CALLS EVIL

But he was an evil king, for he did not
seek the LORD with all his heart.
2 Chronicles 12:14 NLT

As I read the stories of the kings in the Old Testament, I am often amazed at how irresponsibly these men behaved. Reading the accounts of David and his descendants, I am saddened at how often these God-appointed leaders rejected the very One who placed them in their positions of authority.

David, whom the Bible describes as "a man after God's own heart" was adulterous, a disconnected father whose sons rebelled in response to his lack of involvement in their lives. David's son Solomon took the throne next, and is known as the wisest man who ever lived. And yet we find that for all his wisdom, Solomon couldn't follow the Lord's simple instructions NOT to intermarry with foreign women, and so he fell into idolatry.

Now Solomon's son, Rehoboam has come on the scene, and in his arrogance he rejects the counsel of experienced advisors. As a result, ten of the tribes of Israel reject him as their king, and the nation of Israel is divided. Ultimately, due to Rehoboam's poor leadership, the kingdom of Judah is attacked by the king of Egypt. But the Bible says in verse 12 that, *"Because Rehoboam humbled himself, the LORD's anger was turned aside, and he did not destroy him completely. And there was still goodness in the land of Judah."* When I read this, I think this shows a change of heart in Rehoboam, but then I come to verse 14, and God declares him "evil".

What is sobering in this story is the reason the Bible says he was evil. For all of his irresponsibility and poor leadership, this king is recorded as humbling himself and repenting. The Bible doesn't tell us that he married a bunch of foreign women and fell into idolatry like his father did. The Bible doesn't give account of his falling into adultery and murder like his grandfather did. And yet, Rehoboam is the one identified as an evil king!

The scripture says, *"he was an evil king, for he did not seek the LORD with all his heart."* As I read this, I can't help but feel a little concerned about my own spiritual condition. I love the Lord, I would say with all my heart, but I know that there are times when my actions indicate otherwise. All too often, I get caught up in the cares of this world. There are days when I get up and immediately get caught up in the busy-ness of life on earth without taking the time to seek the face of God through prayer and time in His Word. Sometimes, I just simply hold back, whether out of fear or selfishness or misplaced priorities...

Rehoboam was considered EVIL because he did not seek the Lord with all of his heart. I do not want this to be said of me! I do not want to be remembered by God as one who was evil.

As I look at these accounts of the kings, it would seem that God looks at things a bit differently than we do. It was not David's actions that made him "a man after God's own heart." It was not Solomon's actions that made him a wise king, loved by God. And it was not Rehoboam's actions that made him an evil king. As

God told Samuel the prophet at the beginning of this dynasty, *"the LORD does not see as man sees; for man looks at the outward appearance, but the LORD looks at the heart." (1 Samuel 16:7)*

It is your heart God is most concerned with. When He has our hearts, ultimately, He can bring our actions into alignment with His Word. If He does not have our hearts, we will be prone to evil...

Does God have your heart today?

TO SUFFER LOSS

Look at the birds. They don't plant or harvest or store
food in barns, for your heavenly Father feeds them. And
aren't you far more valuable to him than they are?
Matthew 6:26 NLT

I have been an observer in a heart-breaking drama this week. Please bear with me as I attempt to sort through this matter...

While setting up for a VBS/KidzKrusade on Sunday, a nasty thunderstorm blew through. After the rains and wind had subsided, one little robin family had suffered great loss. On the sidewalk beside our bus lay two tiny newly hatched robins and the remains of at least two other eggs. One of the babies lay dead on the cement; the other was badly injured, but still alive. From a distance away, the mother bird watched as we surveyed the situation. We looked up into the tree to see if it might be possible to return the surviving baby to its nest, but the nest was dangling sideways from a branch of the tree. Realizing that there was nothing we could do, we carefully moved the injured bird from the sidewalk to a soft patch of grass beneath the tree. We thought perhaps the mother might find a way to protect and comfort her little one. Sadly, another storm came through a few minutes later, sending what remained of the nest crashing to the sidewalk. When we headed out for the final time that evening, we stopped to check on the little survivor, only to find that ants had overtaken it and killed it.

A few tears were shed as we observed this little tragedy played out before our eyes that day. My heart went out to that little mama who, in a matter of a few minutes, lost everything. And though I know that birds are not emotional or spiritual beings who experience loss as we do, I couldn't help but grieve this great loss on behalf of the mother robin. I continued to think of her throughout the evening and on into the next day. When we arrived at the church on Monday afternoon, the fallen nest still remained on the sidewalk, a sad reminder of the previous day's tragic turn of events.

The most heart-breaking moment, though, came Tuesday evening. A few yards from the fallen nest sat a little robin, fluttering about, chattering a mournful little song. She seemed so lost! Just two days earlier, her little life had great joy and purpose - new little hatchlings greeting the world, needing her constant care and attention. But now, this little mother seemed unable to figure out what to do with herself. With no babies to care for and no nest to go home to, she seemed to have lost her purpose.

I never have been very good at accepting the hard truths of nature. I HATE to watch the documentaries where the cheetah actually catches the poor little rabbit for a meal. I still cry when I watch The Lion King and Mufasa is trampled by the wildebeests. So you can imagine, the Robin Family Saga will not soon be forgotten.

As I have thought about how sad this whole incident made me feel, I was reminded that I was not the only one impacted by this loss. Even this seemingly insignificant incident did not go unnoticed by our heavenly Father who feeds and cares even for the birds. A little part of me wondered why He didn't choose to save this little robin family. He could have...

And I was reminded that His ways are not our ways! Tragedy is a part of life. It is unpleasant, but it is inevitable. It is the "in your face" evidence of our sin-stricken world. It simply cannot be avoided.

I learned today of a human mom who lost her baby, and my heart aches even more deeply than before. Life is hard. There is simply no getting around it. But I am reminded that even in the difficult times, we have a God who cares. Though He may not reverse all the tragedies of life or insulate us from the painful consequences of life in a sin-ridden world, He will never leave us to face the difficult times alone. It is often in these deeply sorrowful times that we can learn to know Him as the "God of all comfort".

Whatever loss may have come your way recently, I want to encourage you with this incredible knowledge that the God who cares for the birds and the flowers, cares even more deeply for you. He will not leave you to face difficult days alone.

NEW PERSPECTIVE
ON WAITING

When the people saw how long it was taking Moses to come back down the mountain, they gathered around Aaron. "Come on," they said, "make us some gods who can lead us. We don't know what happened to this fellow Moses, who brought us here from the land of Egypt."
Exodus 32:1 NLT

T his is the beginning of a story that has always puzzled me. I have never been able to fathom what would entice God's people to turn from him so quickly, or why they would ask Aaron to make them an idol that they could worship. I have always had sort of a "righteous indignation" about this whole episode in the history of Israel.

As I have been studying through the story of the Exodus, I have become even more puzzled by the behavior of the children of Israel than ever. As I have read how the Lord made allowances for the people's faithlessness, how they continually tested His patience, how they grumbled and complained, and whined... I haven't really been able to muster up much sympathy for them. And as I came to the story of the golden calf, and I looked at Aaron's behavior there, I admit, I was almost angry at Aaron! I mean, was he really that stupid? The people had heard the actual voice of God. Aaron had actually been up on the lower part of the mountain for an up close, personal encounter with the Lord (Exodus 24:10-11)! But while God was giving Moses instructions about how he was to ordain Aaron for an important role in ministry, Aaron was becoming the people's leader in idol worship.

But today, I am looking at that account again, and I am beginning to muster a little compassion for Aaron and the people. I think maybe I am beginning to understand a little how it may have been for the children of Israel.

They are waiting. After a lifetime of slavery and oppression, God, with many great signs and wonders, delivered them from oppression. He went ahead of them, showing them the way, taking them on a journey to "the Promised Land". But they're not in the Promised Land yet. They can't see it. They know God is powerful, but they're sitting out in the wilderness now... just waiting.

The Bible says that Moses was up on the mountain for forty days and forty nights. I've never thought of that as being a very long time before... But that's nearly six weeks! That was an entire grading period when I was in school! A lot can happen in six weeks!

And so today, I look back at this story with new understanding. I've been waiting on God lately. I thought He was taking me to the Promised Land, and it seems He has taken me to the wilderness. I was sure that I heard His voice. It was clear. There were no doubts. But an interesting thing happens over time... as you sit at the base of the mountain, just waiting to see what will happen next... You begin to look around. You start to second-guess yourself. Was it REALLY the voice of God you heard? Has all of this been some kind of mistake? How long can I really sit here waiting? Don't I need to get up and get busy DOING something? I mean, if God's not ready to do something here, maybe I need to go somewhere else and look for Him...

Don't worry! I'm not about to go off and build myself a golden calf! But I am understanding better what prompted the children of Israel to do such a thing. I can read the rest of their story and see that God did eventually take them to the Promised Land. He always did have their best interest at heart. They would pay the price for their disobedience, but never did God forsake them. He walked with them. He waited with them. He showed them the way.

Lord, as I am waiting, help me to wait in confidence. Keep me from doing something stupid, Lord! Help me to rest in what I know, and not try to get ahead of You or try to make things happen on my own. I want to make this journey YOUR way!

If you find yourself waiting today, be encouraged. God has not forsaken you. Don't you give up on Him!

GOD MOVES IN
THE DARK TIMES

The Lord went ahead of them. He guided them during the day with a pillar of cloud, and he provided light at night with a pillar of fire. This allowed them to travel by day or by night. And the Lord did not remove the pillar of cloud or pillar of fire from its place in front of the people.
Exodus 13:21-22 NLT

So as the sun began to rise, Moses raised his hand over the sea, and the water rushed back into its usual place. The Egyptians tried to escape, but the Lord swept them into the sea.
Exodus 14:27 NLT

The children of Israel had just left Egypt. They were leaving behind the only life they had ever known - a life of oppression and slavery. They were embarking on a new life - life as a free people in a land God had prepared for them. What an exciting time this must have been for them!

Exciting... but frightening as well. Change is a hard thing. Sometimes it seems easier to just stick with what you know. It may be unpleasant, but at least it's familiar.

So now the children of Israel are out of Egypt and they are on their way to the "Promised Land". They didn't have a fancy GPS system, but they didn't need one. They had God. And God had promised to go ahead of them and to guide them. He went ahead of them in two very visible forms - the pillar of cloud for the day and the pillar of fire for the night.

Did you ever really think about that? I've read it many times, but never really caught it: *This allowed them to travel by day **or by night**.* God provided the pillar of fire so they could travel at night!

I sometimes like to travel at night. I kind of like to see city lights at night. At Christmas time, I love to see all the festive light displays. But most of the time, I much prefer to travel during the day. It's easier to stay awake. It's easier to see where you are going... I've been on dark roads in the middle of nowhere at night, and that is just no fun! It's hard to tell where you are, and you find yourself wondering if you've made a wrong turn, or if you'd even know it if you did make a wrong turn.

So the children of Israel had been traveling, and they stopped and set up camp in a nice, scenic location. They're hanging out at the beach, enjoying a break from the road, taking in a nice sunset... and then they see Pharaoh's army coming! They panic, and suddenly that nice beachfront property just looks like a trap - until God intervenes. The pillar of cloud settles down in between the Israelites and the Egyptians, and as darkness falls, the cloud turns to fire. Feeling safe for the moment, the children of Israel now get to witness a truly amazing miracle - God parts the Red Sea for them. The wind blows, and ground dries out on the seabed, and the people walk right through - during the night. We know that it was night because it's just before dawn that the Lord throws the Egyptians (who are now pursuing the Israelites through the sea) into confusion. And the Bible tells us that just as the sun began to rise, the waters closed back in, killing the entire army of Pharaoh.

This all happened in the night. This miraculous deliverance took place in darkness. But God had made a way for the people to follow Him, even in the dark times.

We may not have a pillar of fire to follow through the dark times of life, but God has not abandoned us to our enemies. He has provided us with all we need to make it through the night.

Your word is a lamp for my feet, a light on my path. Psalm 119:105 NLT

Maybe you are in one of those dark times in your life. I want to encourage you today that God has given you His light that stands between you and the enemy. His Word will give you the direction you are seeking. Set your eyes on His Word, and then step out in faith. He will show you which way to go.

You don't have to cower down in the darkness. Just look up - He's lighting the way!

AUDIBLE

Then the Lord said to Moses, "I will come to you in a thick cloud, Moses, so the people themselves can hear me when I speak with you. Then they will always trust you."

Exodus 19:9 NLT

Then God gave the people all these instructions...

When the people heard the thunder and the loud blast of the ram's horn, and when they saw the flashes of lightning and the smoke billowing from the mountain, they stood at a distance, trembling with fear. And they said to Moses, "You speak to us, and we will listen. But don't let God speak directly to us, or we will die!"

Exodus 20:1, 18-19 NLT

I have often wished the Lord would just speak to me in an audible voice! I mean, sometimes I just get so frustrated as I go along in life, wondering where to turn, which way to go... And I cry out to God asking for direction. Sometimes, I get a very clear answer. Other times, He just says, "Trust Me," and I am called to walk by faith. Lately, I have struggled with fear, wondering if I am somehow misunderstanding or misinterpreting what God is saying to me. I wish He would just speak clearly from heaven!

Well... that's what I THINK I want...

The children of Israel got that chance! But they didn't appreciate it. God spoke so that they could hear His voice, and rather than listening to what He said to them, the people got so overcome with fear that they begged Moses to ask God to stop. They didn't want to hear his voice anymore.

I had never realized this before, but did you know that God actually gave the Ten Commandments in the hearing of the children of Israel? He told Moses to go get the people ready - to instruct them on how to prepare for this wonderful opportunity. He told them where to stand, and when to go there (on the third day...!). And then He gave them instructions. These were pretty straight-forward instructions - nothing too complicated. If the people had simply listened when God spoke, they could have been saved much heartache in the years that followed! But they stood at a distance, trembling with fear, and they completely missed what God wanted to say to them because they valued their lives above God.

"Oh Moses! Don't let God talk to us that way! We're scared of Him! We'd rather hear your version of what God wants to say!"

We look down on the children of Israel for their reaction, but isn't that exactly what we do today? God has given us His Word. He has spoken very clearly to us from it. But we feign confusion, and inexperience, and lack of education. We would much rather someone else read His Word for us and tell us what it says so we don't have to listen directly to the voice of God. We would rather read books by Christian authors than the Book by the Author of Christianity!

God wanted the people to hear His voice at Sinai. I believe He wants us to hear His voice today. Maybe it's time we stop making excuses and playing dumb. Maybe it's really not as hard a thing as we have made it. Maybe - just maybe - God is speaking and we are cowering.

Have I done that? Have I so valued my own life, my own plans, my own dreams, my own "stuff" that when God wanted to speak to me I covered my ears and cowered down, using fear as an excuse to remain ignorant of the ways of God? I pray that would no longer be the case.

Come near to God and hear His voice. He wants to speak, if only we will listen.

It may be a little scary, but listen carefully.

READY FOR BATTLE

*When Pharaoh let the people go, God did not lead them
by way of the land of the Philistines, although that
was near. For God said, "Lest the people change their
minds when they see war and return to Egypt." But
God led the people around by the way of the wilderness
toward the Red Sea. And the people of Israel went
up out of the land of Egypt equipped for battle.*
Exodus 13:17-18 NLT

T he Exodus of the children of Israel out of Egypt is such an
incredible account! Before they ever left Egypt, God had
revealed Himself in so many powerful ways, and He had
made it very clear whose side He was on. Though many terrors
came upon Egypt, in the land of Goshen where the children of Israel were living, scripture tells us that the people were protected
from at least some of the plagues. And now they were free, having
walked right out of Egypt because God had delivered them!

Now they are on their way to the Promised Land, and God is leading them. The Bible says that they were prepared for the battle.
(Some translations state that the people marched out of Egypt in

battle formation.) God could have taken them the short way, but the Bible tells us that He took them the long way. Why? Because He knew they might turn back if they were faced with the prospect of war. So even though the people may have thought they were ready for battle, the Lord protected them from this test of their faith. They would face plenty of challenges later on, and they would eventually need those battle preparations, but for now, God took them around the battle.

I am reminded of the old cartoons here... I picture the little guy who thinks he's big, marching out to meet his opponent, armed with a little cork gun. But behind this little guy is a big guy, holding onto his shirttails, keeping his little friend from getting into a fight he's not really ready for...

I think there is an important lesson to be learned here. God wants us to be prepared. He's given us spiritual armor for our protection and His Word as a weapon. When the battle comes, He wants us to be ready. Fortunately, God loves us and cares for us and often takes us around the battle. He protects us from those things He knows we aren't ready for. But He wants us prepared!

Whatever trial you're facing today, I want to encourage you: God is aware of your situation. It has not taken Him by surprise. He could have taken you around the battle. If He hasn't, He must know that you are ready, even though you may not feel like it. But trust His love for you. He has already given you what you need for the battle, and He will stand with you and fight.

If you are not in the battle today, thank God for protecting you from it. Enjoy the time of rest, but don't become complacent, thinking God will always take you around the Philistines of life. Take this time to get prepared. Put on that armor. Draw your sword. Get used to the feel of it, because the day is coming when you're going to need it, so be ready!

If it seems like God is taking you the long way around today, do not be discouraged. Maybe you're tired of waiting. Maybe it seems like He's being slow to answer. I want to encourage you: walk patiently with Him through this time, comforted with the knowledge that He knows what you're ready for.

A final word: Be strong in the Lord and in his mighty power. Put on all of God's armor so that you will be able to stand firm against all strategies of the devil. For we are not fighting against flesh-and-blood enemies, but against evil rulers and authorities of the unseen world, against mighty powers in this dark world, and against evil spirits in the heavenly places.
Therefore, put on every piece of God's armor so you will be able to resist the enemy in the time of evil. Then after the battle you will still be standing firm. Stand your ground, putting on the belt of truth and the body armor of God's righteousness. For shoes, put on the peace that comes from the Good News so that you will be fully prepared. In addition to all of these, hold up the shield of faith to stop the fiery arrows of the devil. Put on salvation as your helmet, and take the sword of the Spirit, which is the word of God. Ephesians 6:10-17 NLT

LEARNING TO LISTEN

This is what the Lord says - the Lord who made the earth, who formed and established it, whose name is the Lord: Ask me and I will tell you remarkable secrets you do not know about things to come.
Jeremiah 33:2-3 NLT

I have been full of questions lately. A lot of those questions start with "why...". It has been a confusing time, a time when I have tried to figure things out. I have been somewhat unsuccessful in these efforts, and have been left feeling frustrated and confused.

I've actually been a little upset at God about this. But it's not His fault. He doesn't want me confused. He is not trying to frustrate me. He is quite willing for me to know the truth, but I think it is just that I am having a hard time listening. After all, He did say, "Ask me and I will tell you..."

I don't sit still very well. The joke is that if I sit still for too long, I fall asleep - and that is not far from the truth. I get caught up in this whirlwind of activity, not realizing until later that I am accomplishing nothing. By the end of the day I am exhausted, but as I try to figure out why, it all seems so futile. It's like all my efforts were in vain. And as I drop into bed at night, I am almost instantly asleep. I never remember much past turning off the light - and sometimes I don't even remember that!

God is calling me to be still... But there is just so much that needs to be done! I don't have time to sit still!

"Be still and know..." But I CAN'T be still because I know... how much there is to do and how little time there is to accomplish it!

"Be still and know that I am God." Could it really be that simple? He wouldn't have said it if it wasn't true. He is God. He is capable of taking care of all of those things I am concerning myself with. He is GOD! What is so complicated about that? It's the letting go... Trusting... I've been asking, but I haven't been waiting for Him to answer. That's got to change!

"Be still..."

It's time to listen...

ON THE ROAD AGAIN...

The Lord went ahead of them. He guided them
during the day with a pillar of cloud, and he
provided light at night with a pillar of fire. This
allowed them to travel by day or by night.
Exodus 13:21 NLT

I t's one of those seasons... Nothing seems to make sense...
What I thought was the right direction was apparently the
wrong direction... What I thought was the wrong direction
was apparently the right direction! Anybody else ever have those
times?

I'm beginning to understand, on a small scale, what the children
of Israel must have been feeling as they left Egypt. They had seen
the mighty hand of God at work, miraculously delivering them
from slavery, setting them free to pursue what looked to be a
very bright future. So they're on their way to the Promised Land.
They're following God, and maybe don't even realize that God is
taking them on a round-about kind of journey to their destination. So they're following the pillar of cloud by day and the pillar
of fire by night, and they know they are on the right path because

they are following God. Then, all of a sudden, God pulls a u-turn on them because He's working on a plan to show His glory to Pharaoh. But still the children of Israel follow - no problem!

There they are, all camped out where God said to camp. They're happy. They're content. They're just waiting for God to tell them to go, and then they'll be on their way. But they look up and see that Pharaoh's army is after them! Then they look the other way, and suddenly that sweet beachfront property they're camped on doesn't look so sweet anymore! Now they're panicking. They're crying and complaining because, understandably, they're scared to death!

I can relate, and maybe you can, too. I thought God was leading in a certain direction. It was exciting, looking to the future, wondering exactly what the road would look like, but exciting because God was in it. I was following God, but soon realized we weren't going the direct route, so I figured there must be "Philistines" out there He was protecting me from. That's okay. I'm ready for the journey, as long as God's leading the way. But then came the u-turn, and that was almost more exciting because it seemed He had spoken so clearly, "Camp here."

But then, somehow, here I am - Pharaoh's army is behind me, and the Red Sea lies ahead, and even though I know how the biblical account turns out, I confess I'm feeling a little panicky.

I've told you before how I prefer the big-picture of the road map to the turn-by-turn instructions of a GPS... Well... God's taking me on a GPS journey! I'm following the pillar of cloud, but I'm frustrated because I can't see past it - all I can see is the cloud. But God is in the cloud! And that's got to be enough! He is MORE than enough!

So step by step, putting one foot in front of the other, following God even though I'm not quite sure where we're going or how we're getting there, I'm hitting the road again...

A wise pastor once told me that it's easier for God to steer a moving vessel... Well, I'm moving. Lord - steer away!

So if you find yourself adrift, like a ship with no direction, I want to encourage you to get in motion, then let the Lord lead the way, learning to trust your Captain even when you can't see the shore. I'm right there with you - just along for the ride!

WHY GOD ANSWERS
PRAYER

*Hear my prayer, O Lord; listen to my plea! Answer
me because you are faithful and righteous.*
Psalm 143:1 NLT

I don't know about you, but I tend to spend a lot of time asking
God for things. I wake up in the morning asking Him for a
good day (and usually putting in my request for some sunshine). I go along through the day asking for His guidance and
provision. I ask for His protection and for wisdom. I ask for silly
things and selfish things and things of no real significance in the
grand scheme of eternity. I ask, and I ask, and I ask...

The problem is not in the asking, because God has told us in His
Word that we should ask. And as I often point out to the Lord (as if

He has forgotten!), He did say in James, "You have not because you ask not...).

The problem comes when I begin to think that I deserve an answer. God does answer prayer, and I am so thankful for that. He is concerned about the little details of my life. He LOVES me! That is so incredible! But His answers to my prayers do not come because I am so spiritual. His answers are not in response to my being kind or right or deserving in any way. The answers are simply about who God is.

David understood this simple truth, pouring out his heart, and crying out to God for help. He cried out to God not because he thought he deserved an answer, but because he had an understanding of the nature of God. David didn't ask God to answer because he (David) was good, but because HE (God) was good: "because YOU are faithful and righteous".

It kind of brings a new perspective to my prayer life, this understanding that God's response to my prayer is not about me...

Thank You, God, that You remain faithful even when I am faithless. Thank You that Your answers to my prayers are based on how good You are and not on how good I am. Now please teach me to do Your will (v.10)...

Just because... He is faithful and righteous.

THE EXPENDABLES

He is the God who made the world and everything in it.
Since he is Lord of heaven and earth, he doesn't live in
man-made temples, and human hands can't serve his
needs - for he has no needs. He himself gives life and
breath to everything, and he satisfies every need.
Acts 17:24-25 NLT

I have a tendency to overextend myself... just a little! I look around at what needs to be done, and though I may sometimes get a little overwhelmed, I manage to convince myself that I need to make sure that everything gets done. After all, if I don't do it, who will?

There's a statistic I hear around the church very often: "20% of the people do 80% of the work in the church"(or is it "10% of the people do 90% of the work"?)...

The theory here is that a few committed people manage to get done most of what happens in the local church and that the rest are uncommitted slackers. There is some definite truth to that, because I think one of the greatest shortcomings in modern "Christianity" is a lack of commitment. (In truth, I fear that what really is happening is that a large percentage of modern church-goers are not really saved, but that is a matter for another day!)

Among those 10-20 percent who fall into the "committed worker" category in the church, there is a different problem I have observed. Those workers (among whom I number myself) often fall into the trap of believing that they are irreplaceable. We often commit to much more than we actually have time to do. We may commit to things that we absolutely don't want to do, taking on a martyr attitude, and making sure people know what a sacrifice we are making "to do the work of the Lord." We think that if we stop what we are doing, the kingdom of God may just come crumbling down!

Now, I don't want to imply that the things we do for the Lord do not matter, because that is absolutely NOT the case. But what I think we often fail to understand is that while God desires that we would serve Him with all our hearts, this is really more for us than it is for Him. He does not NEED us! He's GOD, remember? He can do ANYTHING He wants, ANY WAY He wants, and He does not NEED my help (or my permission!). As Paul pointed out to his listeners at Mars Hill, "...*human hands can't serve his needs, for he has no needs.*"

So what I want to encourage you today, especially at this time of year when a few people find themselves taking on all the "seasonal work" of the church, overextending themselves, getting stressed out, or feeling guilty that they are not doing enough...

Relax!

Stop trying to run everything yourself, on your own strength. Take time to seek the face of God. Rest in His loving arms. Let His Spirit lead you in the works He would have you do. Then do those things joyfully, out of your love for a Savior who came to earth as a baby and gave His life for you, and not out of guilt or obligation.

God wants you to love Him, but He does not need you to work for Him. He understands that your true love for Him will motivate you to service.

Understanding that He is a big, powerful God, and I am, in a sense, expendable, leaves me much freedom: freedom to love Him more fully, and thereby to minister more effectively.

WHAT THE ONE WHO FORMED YOU SAYS...

But now, O Jacob, listen to the Lord who created you. O Israel, the one who formed you says, "Do not be afraid, for I have ransomed you. I have called you by name; you are mine. When you go through deep waters, I will be with you. When you go through rivers of difficulty, you will not drown. When you walk through the fires of oppression, you will not be burned up; the flames will not consume you... you are precious to me. You are honored, and I love you. Do not be afraid, for I am with you..."
Isaiah 43:1-5 NLT

L ife has been a little crazy lately. Actually, that's not really the half of it! I have felt stretched beyond belief, weary in ways I never knew possible, fearful of the future.

Life is a series of changes, I know, but lately I just long for things to be still - to calm down, if only for a moment. I find myself looking for perspective, to find some way to make sense out of confusion... I feel like I'm flying blind, moving forward at warp speed but navigation is offline, so I wait for the inevitable crash...

But it doesn't come. The crash does not come, because in spite of what I FEEL, life is not out of control because my Father has promised to be with me. I may say things are a mess, but here is what HE says:

"Do not be afraid."

"I have called you by name."

"You are mine."

"I will be with you."

"You will not drown."

"You will not be burned up."

"You are precious to me."

"I love you."

"I am with you."

I am so encouraged to know that the same God who formed Israel also formed me; that the same God who said to His children in times past, "I love you," says the same to me today.

Maybe you can relate to how I've been feeling. Maybe life seems to you a confusing mess. Be encouraged today that the God who formed you has promised to be with you. Enjoy a little rest in His strong arms today.

"You are precious..."

THE TRAGEDY
OF WASTED
OPPORTUNITY

*And because of their unbelief, he couldn't do any
mighty miracles among them except to place his
hands on a few sick people and heal them.*
Mark 6:5 NLT

I think this may be one of the saddest verses I have ever read in the Bible.

Jesus had gone home for a visit. You would think the people of Nazareth would have been watching Jesus' travels with keen interest. I mean, He was "one of their own".

The hometown boy was making quite a name with all the amazing miracles He was performing. And now He was coming home. They could have met Him with a parade, or a supper in His honor...

That was not the case. Jesus came home, and hung around for a few days. Then the Sabbath came along, so He went to the synagogue to teach. Initially, the people were amazed. But then they began to talk among themselves, and before long, the Scriptures say, *"They were deeply offended and refused to believe in him"* (v.3).

What a tragedy!

I wonder what it was that Jesus had planned for His family and His hometown? I can only imagine that it was something wonderful. After all, this is Jesus we're talking about! Who knows what incredible things might have happened?!

We can recognize that what Jesus did do in Nazareth was pretty incredible - He healed the sick. To us, this is big! But what we see in Scripture is that this didn't even scratch the surface of what Jesus wanted to do there. "Because of their unbelief..."

I wonder what mighty miracles we might be seeing now that we are missing because of unbelief?

The same Jesus that wanted to do mighty miracles in His own hometown is waiting to move mightily in our lives as well.

What an incredible opportunity is set before us! I pray that I will not miss out like the people of Nazareth did...

WHAT ARE YOU LOOKING AT?

So we don't look at the troubles we can see now;
rather, we fix our gaze on things that cannot be
seen. For the things we see now will soon be gone,
but the things we cannot see will last forever.
2 Corinthians 4:18 NLT

One look around is often all it takes for discouragement to enter the scene.

Now, I like to think of myself as a "glass half full" kind of girl, but I have to confess that can be a little hard when the glass looks nine-tenths empty! You know how it is... The numbers stack up a bit higher on the bill side than the income side... Or maybe it's relationship troubles... Or dissatisfaction at work or school... Or something altogether different.

Circumstances can be discouraging at times!

I'm pretty sure the apostle Paul would agree with me. I mean, if ever a person had endured difficult circumstances, Paul was the guy. Arrested over and over again... Imprisoned... Shipwrecked - three times! And if all that wasn't enough, the treatment he got from his "friends" and "supporters" would be enough to send anyone over the edge!

He poured his life into churches, only to have them turn on him, criticize him, and just generally aggravate him... If Paul had just taken a moment to consider his circumstances, he would certainly have been within his rights to throw the world's biggest pity party!

But he looked beyond his circumstances.

He didn't just look toward the day when he might be free from imprisonment. He wasn't hoping for a time when his circumstances would improve. Paul was focused on things that could not be seen with physical eyes.

He had an *internal* perspective - looking to the Spirit of God within him for the peace He came to give.

And Paul had an *eternal* perspective - he was looking to the day that he would put off his physical body with all of its suffering and troubles and be united with Christ in heaven forever.

We still reap the benefits of Paul's perspective on life. He left us many God-inspired words to instruct and encourage us along this journey of life on earth.

Lord, make me more like Paul, that I may look past the troubles I can see, to the things of Your Spirit that will last forever...

NEW VISION

When the servant of the man of God got up early the next morning and went outside, there were troops, horses, and chariots everywhere. "Oh, sir, what will we do now?" the young man cried to Elisha. "Don't be afraid!" Elisha told him. "For there are more on our side than on theirs!" Then Elisha prayed, "O Lord, open his eyes and let him see!" The Lord opened the young man's eyes, and when he looked up, he saw that the hillside around Elisha was filled with horses and chariots of fire.
2Kings 6:15-17 NLT

When circumstances look bleak, it can be easy to panic. It's not necessarily that we lose faith. Sometimes, it's just being realistic.

It's not that we don't believe God CAN deliver us. We just don't know if He WILL or if maybe He's got some lessons for us in the circumstances.

This is where Elisha's servant was on this particular morning. He hadn't gone out looking for trouble. But when he went out, there it was! He was surrounded by the enemy. That had to be a little scary!

The key to this story, though, is not found in what the servant could see. It was in what he COULDN'T see.

The circumstances looked BAD - there was no denying that fact. But beyond the circumstances, something else was going on, and God had it all under control!

As we look around at our lives and our circumstances, it can be easy to feel overwhelmed. From where we're standing, it's easy to see the opposition. It looks like we're all alone in the situation.

That's how it looked to Elisha's servant, too. For all he knew it as just him and Elisha against a multitude of armed troops. But when God opened his eyes, it all looked different!

My prayer for you today is that in the midst of whatever circumstance you find yourself, that God would open your eyes... That He would give you new vision to see beyond the circumstances to His provision.

With God on your side, the opposition is outnumbered.

Rest today in that knowledge, and ask the Lord for new vision.

INVISIBILITY...

It was by faith that Moses left the land of Egypt,
not fearing the king's anger. He kept right on going
because he kept his eyes on the one who is invisible.
Hebrews 11:27 NLT

A s I read this verse this morning, my first thought was to laugh. I mean, really, how do you keep your eyes on someone who is invisible? But then I was intrigued. How DO you keep your eyes on One who is invisible?

This verse leaves me thinking of old television shows and movies about the "Invisible Man". It reminds me of a particular episode of Star Trek where an "invisible" force was creating havoc on the Enterprise. It's a great concept for science fiction, but this is NOT science fiction - it's REALITY.

So, the question, "How do you keep your eyes on the one who is invisible?" is a very important question, indeed. The Bible tells us that Moses did it, so we know it is not an impossible task.

I think it was on an old Tom & Jerry cartoon that Jerry Mouse, trying to hide from Tom Cat painted himself with invisible ink. Jerry took full advantage of the opportunity to terrorize Tom, aided greatly by the fact that Tom could not see him. Somewhere along the way, though, Jerry wandered through a mud puddle or something, and even though he was still invisible, he left a trail of footprints that Tom could follow.

Jesus has left an amazing set of footprints for us to follow!

He's given us His Word - the Bible - full of very clear and useful information as to the Person of Jesus Christ and His will for our lives. He has set an example for us, that though we may not physically see Him, we can see where He has been and know the direction that He wants us to go.

It won't always be easy, but God never calls us to do the impossible.

"For God called you to do good, even if it means suffering, just as Christ suffered for you. He is your example, and you must follow in his steps." 1 Peter 2:21

Like Moses, I want to walk in faith, keeping my eyes on the One who is invisible. It may not make sense to those who are watching... They may think me a little crazy, but that's okay. I know Who I'm following, and I trust that He knows where we're going!

So keep your eyes on the Invisible...

JARS OF CLAY

We now have this light shining in our hearts, but we ourselves are like fragile clay jars containing this great treasure. This makes it clear that our great power is from God, not from ourselves.
2 Corinthians 4:7 NLT

It's April and nowhere near time to be thinking about Halloween, but this verse made me think about jack-o-lanterns. That's funny, because we don't really "do" Halloween...!

But this verse is a continuation of the passage in 2 Corinthians 3 where Paul is referencing the story of Moses' encounter with God on the mountain. It is one of my favorite stories in the Bible and one of the foundational elements behind my Invisible Woman blog - that what would be seen in me is not me but Him.

So Moses had gone up to the mountain to receive the Law from the Lord. He stayed a while (40 days and nights) and then came down shining.

The people were frightened by the glowing Moses, but that wonderful glow was just the natural result of time spent in the presence of God. It was not for Moses' glory, but for God's glory.

Moses had no agenda here - no dreams of fame for the light in him. He understood that the light had nothing to do with him, but was all about Who he had been with.

So Paul points out that the Light that was reflected in Moses' face is the same Light that inhabits the Christian. It is not a light that we can boast of having turned on. It has nothing to do with us, but rather is all about Who is within us.

As a clay pot that will slip from my hands and shatter into a million pieces, that jar is not what is valuable in showing forth the light.

Or like that jack-o-lantern, which may be intricately carved to allow the light to shine through, we understand that the pumpkin is not the source of the light, but is merely the container for the light. The pumpkin will eventually rot but the light source remains...

And so it is that whatever light shines forth from my life is not from me, but radiates from the Spirit of God within me.

It is not my light, but His.

Not my power, but His power.

Only for His glory and never for mine.

WHAT'S IT GOING TO TAKE?

*I am in them and you are in me. May they experience
such perfect unity that the world will know that you
sent me and that you love them as much as you love me.*
John 17:23 NLT

This weekend we enjoyed leading an unusual service. The Baptist, Methodist, and Assembly of God churches all got together for a Sunday evening service. We had a blast!

What is sad is that this IS unusual. Modern denominationalism has got a lot of people very mixed up about the ways of the Lord. It often seems as if churches believe that they are in competition with one another! And this is no friendly competition either. It's like they're out for blood! Is it any wonder that we are seeing such a decline in the church in America?

On the night that he was betrayed, Jesus left US instructions about how we were to live. These instructions were for the church that had not even officially started yet. His words were part of a prayer to the Father on behalf of His disciples - Present (the twelve) and future (us!).

In John 17:20, He specifically identifies who He is praying for: "*not only for these disciples, but for ALL who will EVER believe in me through their message*" (emphasis mine).

So if Jesus cared enough to spend His final hours on earth praying for us, what He was saying must have been important. There was an urgency to His words, because He knew His time on earth was short, but His message needed to continue even when He was no longer physically present on earth.

So what was so important to Jesus that He devoted His last hours to praying for us?

Was it that He wanted all of His followers to go to Bible college and seminary so that they could be properly equipped to share His Word? Was it that He wanted them to build big, beautiful buildings for people to gather in worship? Was it that He wanted the coming church to provide cutting edge programming for people of all ages? Was it stewardship programs, or committee meetings, or church suppers?

No.

It was none of these things.

What Jesus devoted His final hours to was not what most modern churches are devoting their time and attention to. And yet, if we would just look at what our Lord said, He has given us the key to building an effective church:

"*... May they experience such perfect unity that the world will know that you sent me and that you love them...*"

The way the world will be able to know that God sent Jesus is by the unity of the believers. Is it any wonder that people find little need of the church today?

What we need is not another program, or a fancier building, or more cutting edge technology or a different style of music.

If we really want the world to come to Christ - if we want them to know Jesus as Son of God and Savior - if we truly want them to know the love of Jesus - He told us how to make it happen: UNITY.

When the church stops its internal bickering, when we stop this crazy denominational competition, when we all get busy loving one another and bearing one another's burdens... you never know - we might just change our world!

GREAT IS HIS FAITHFULNESS

Great is his faithfulness; his mercies
begin afresh each morning.
Lamentations 3:23 NLT

T he sun is shining this morning. Looks like a beautiful day ahead...

It's not what I was expecting. I fell asleep last night to the sound of pouring rain, and fleeting thoughts of other storms that have passed this way before. It's been like that all week.

As we prepared to travel to the town where we have been ministering this week, I went online to check the weather forecast. I have been feeling rather "sun-deprived" for much of the past year, so I went to the weather website hopeful that things would be looking bright. Things were NOT looking bright. In fact, the forecast called for nice weather in the days up until we arrived, at which point it would begin to rain through the rest of our sched-uled days in this location. Well... at least I didn't come with high expectations of sunshine!

What has happened has been very different from the forecast. Each afternoon, I have had sunshine. And each day I have made sure to get out and go for a walk, because I knew that according to the weather man, it would be short lived. Most nights, there has been rain as I have fallen asleep, but in the morning, I have risen to sunlight streaming through the windows!

As I sit this morning typing this, there is actually a glare coming from the window in front of me, causing me to squint a bit... And it calls me to praise the Lord!

It may seem a small thing, and yet as I bask in the glorious sun-light this morning, all I can think of is the incredible love and faithfulness of my Father!

He has freed me from the "rainy days" of trouble in the past, and let His Light shine down on me, warming my heart and lighting my way.

Great is His faithfulness, indeed!

What a wonderful thought...!

Weeping may last through the night, but joy comes with the morn-ing! Psalm 30:5b

THE BOAT IS
ROCKING...

*Jesus was sleeping at the back of the boat with his head
on a cushion. The disciples woke him up, shouting,
"Teacher, don't you care that we're going to drown?"
When Jesus woke up, he rebuked the wind and said to the
waves, "Silence! Be still!" Suddenly the wind stopped,
and there was a great calm. Then he asked them,
"Why are you afraid? Do you still have no faith?"*
Mark 4:38-40 NLT

Jesus has been healing the sick, casting out demons, teaching about the Kingdom of God. He has confided in His disciples deep truths about Himself and His Father. Now they've started across the lake to take a little break, and Jesus has laid down to catch a nap.

A storm comes up, but honestly, could there be any safer place to be in that storm than in a boat with Jesus? He created the world after all—the lake, the tree of whose wood the boat was made, the disciples themselves.

Could there be any safer place on the planet than right there with Jesus?

Sound familiar?

We're not actually in a boat on a stormy lake. But we find ourselves in "troubled waters". Oftentimes, instead of resting in the knowledge that Jesus is "in the boat with us", don't we, like the disciples, fret and worry that we are going to drown?

If we cannot find safety in the presence of the Creator of the universe, we are truly without hope!

But the truth of the matter is that as the disciples were in perfect safety in the presence of the Lord, so we are safe in the presence of our Lord.

The boat may rock and the waters may come in.

We might even get thrown right out of the boat—this much is true. But whatever it feels like in the midst of the storm, we can rest assured in the knowledge that our eternity is secure through faith in Jesus Christ as Lord.

We are pressed on every side by troubles, but we are not crushed. We are perplexed, but not driven to despair. We are hunted down, but never abandoned by God. We get knocked down, but we are not destroyed. 2 Corinthians 4:8-9

LAYING DOWN
MY RIGHTS

For God is pleased with you when you do what you know
is right and patiently endure unfair treatment.
1 Peter 2:19 NLT

I suffer from a "fairness complex". I think that things should be done fairly. It's the American way, isn't it? We're all about our "rights". We guard them, defend them, fight for them.... to the point that we will violate someone else's rights if we perceive they are getting in the way of our own rights.

It's the American way, certainly, but is it the Christian way? The truth is that it is not, and here's where my struggle comes in.

We have equated fairness with right-ness for so long that we have begun to believe it: what is fair must be right. In truth, we subconsciously know that this line of thinking is incorrect. We all know that life is not fair.

Most, if not all, of us have found ourselves in a situation where there was no "fair" solution. What was good for one was not good for others, or, (pardon my digression into Star Trek rhetoric) "The needs of the many outweigh the needs of the few - or the one." This cannot be said to be fair.

And so, I must come to terms with the fairness myth.

The idea of fairness is a nice thing, but the reality is that it simply does not exist in many situations. But even when things can be done fairly, often they are not. And that is where I must put my faith into action.

I'm glad that it was Peter who was inspired by the Holy Spirit to write these words, because Peter is a guy I can relate to.

Peter could not have come to these conclusions easily - or on his own. After all, Peter is the guy who stood up to defend Jesus at Gethsemane, cutting off the ear of the soldier who had come to arrest his friend and Lord. Peter had been all about fairness for much of his life. Now we see the Lord has shown him a better way.

So Peter instructs us to do what is right, even when we are treated unfairly.

These instructions were specifically given to slaves, and more specifically to slaves with cruel masters. The instructions were further applied to women with ungodly husbands. Modern Christianity would stand to defend the rights of these slaves to their freedom, and the rights of these women to equity in marriage. Biblical Christianity looked upon this situation in a different light. This was an opportunity to live pleasing before God (1 Peter 2:19)... A chance to follow the example of Christ (1 Peter 2:21-24)... An opportunity to win souls not with words but by example (1 Peter 31-2).

And so the question I must ask myself is, "What do I value more?"

Am I more concerned with fairness? Will I stubbornly hold onto my rights at the expense of someone else's soul?

 Or will I hear the words of the Lord through Peter, instructing me to quit worrying about what's fair, quit basing my actions on how someone else is treating me, and simply follow the example of Christ?

MUCH MORE
THAN THIS

Now all glory to God, who is able, through his
mighty power at work within us, to accomplish
infinitely more than we might ask or think.
Ephesians 3:20 NLT

A few years ago, we found ourselves in a once-familiar situation: vehicle problems that threatened to leave us either stranded, "out of business", or ridiculously indebted.

Early in our ministry, this was our almost-daily condition. Breakdowns were common, finances were always lacking, and we were keenly aware that our lifestyle was at best precarious... As the years went on, however, the Lord blessed us with more reliable transportation, while the enemy chose to attack on different fronts.

So, when our alternator went out on this particular occasion, and a little checking around brought us to the reality that just a replacement part was going to cost several times more than what we had in the bank, we were asking that familiar question, "What now?"

We managed to limp the bus into El Paso, Texas, which we were jokingly informed is "the nicest city in Mexico". It is a city to which Jeremiah 29:11 had never been before. We found ourselves literally "in the desert".

We did not know a single person in El Paso. Jeff had spoken on the phone just once with a pastor at a church we'd never been to. The pastor had agreed to let us park the bus in his church parking lot overnight while we were in town for an evening conference. Then vehicle trouble hit and "overnight" turned into "over a week."

So first we began to panic - which was a silly waste of time.

And then we began to pray.

Immediately, the Lord began to work! God's provision, of course, was amazing!

An obscure biblical story was pointed out to me at the beginning of this process that challenged my perspective.

Amaziah, son of Joash, has become the king of Judah. The Bible says, *"Amaziah did what was pleasing in the Lord's sight, but not wholeheartedly."* (2 Chronicles 25:2) This is significant in and of itself, but that is a thought for another day.

What happens is that Amaziah decides to go to war, and because he is not satisfied with the number of his troops, he decides to go over to Israel and hire some more soldiers. God sends a messenger to Amaziah to tell him to send the hired troops home, or else

Amaziah will be defeated in battle. Amaziah asks the very practical question, *"But what about all that silver I paid to hire the army of Israel?"* (2 Chronicles 25:9a)

Amaziah is getting ready for battle. He is the king - the leader of many people.

Amaziah is concerned about the money, but God is concerned about his heart.

God is wanting to teach Amaziah to trust Him instead of trusting in numbers. But Amaziah has already paid out all this money, and he's afraid that it's irresponsible of him to waste those funds.

The lesson God had for Amaziah that day, He's been teaching me this week:
"The LORD is able to give you much more than this!" (2 Chronicles 25:9b)

We underestimate the God of the Universe, don't we? We know that He made everything, that He owns everything, that He is in control of everything... We say that we believe these things, and yet, how often do we, like Amaziah, second-guess the God we claim to trust? "But, God, what about...?"

God says, "Trust Me. I am able to give you much more than this!"

What is it you are holding onto today? What's your "back-up plan" if God doesn't come through the way you're expecting? Could it be that our "Plan B" is nothing but a show of faithlessness?

Maybe it's time to let go of our plans, and trust the One who said, *"I know the plans I have for you..."*

WITH ALL MY HEART

Amaziah did what was pleasing in the Lord's sight, but not wholeheartedly.
2Chronicles 25:2 NLT

What a legacy! To be known throughout the generations as a person who half-heartedly served the Lord... That is not something to aspire to!

The thing is, when the kings of Israel and Judah are discussed, Amaziah is not a name that usually comes up. I'd venture a guess that many Christians don't even know who Amaziah was. And his impact on the world - though good - was limited.

As I consider his story, it seems to me that Amaziah could be the "poster child" for modern American Christianity. I mean, here's this guy. He comes from a good family - his dad was Joash, the famed king of Judah who took office at the ripe old age of seven and served the Lord wholeheartedly throughout most of his lifetime. (Joash had some issues later in life, which led to his demise.) Amaziah comes on the scene, and he's out to follow God. He executes the guys that assassinated his father. He listens initially to the prophets God sends to him. He sees victory as a result of following the Lord.

But then he falls into idolatry, and the people he was charged with leading are the ones who end up getting hurt.

The Bible says, *"Amaziah did what was pleasing in the Lord's sight..."*

Compared to many of the kings who had come before him, Amaziah was a pretty good guy. Compared to many who would come after him, Amaziah did really well.

Amaziah's problem is a common one today - it's the problem of comparison. When we use the world around us as a standard, it's not hard to measure up. Compared to 99% of the people in the world, I may be doing really well, but the thing is - God is not impressed with that. He is not measuring me against the rest of the world. He's not grading on the curve. Doing better than most is NOT good enough, because God measures us against the TRUTH. His standard is righteousness, and even if I'm at the top of the class, I do not measure up.

"...But not wholeheartedly."

This is the thing that cuts me to the core, and calls me to repentance. I'm out here and I'm trying to do what is pleasing in God's sight... I'm trying to serve Him, and I'm singing songs for Him, and I'm talking to people in the church about Him... I'm living kind of a crazy lifestyle for him, packing up my house every few days and moving down the road... But am I really serving Him WHOLE-HEARTEDLY? Too often, I'm afraid the answer is "no."

It's easier to hit the "snooze" in the morning and sleep a few minutes than to get up and spend time with the Lord in prayer. It's easier to pick up a novel and read some good fiction than to pick up my Bible and read. It's easier to put on a video to watch than to spend time studying God's Word...

The day-to-day... I guess this is where the journey really begins - putting it into practice - wholeheartedly doing what is pleasing in the Lord's sight.

I don't want to be like Amaziah, remembered for my mediocrity about the things of God... Do you?

WHEN THE BROOK DRIES UP

So Elijah did as the Lord told him and camped beside Kerith Brook, east of the Jordan. The ravens brought him bread and meat each morning and evening, and he drank from the brook. But after a while the brook dried up, for there was no rainfall anywhere in the land.

1 Kings 17:5-7 NLT

The man of God is being obedient. The Lord gave him instructions and Elijah did exactly as he was told. And as a result, Elijah saw the Lord's provision. Everything Elijah needed was taken care of. For a while.

"But after a while the brook dried up..." Elijah hasn't strayed from

doing what God told him to do. He is still living in obedience to the Lord. He is trusting fully in God's provision.

And the brook dries up.

The Bible doesn't tell us how Elijah responded at this time. It couldn't have been this big surprise for the prophet. I mean, he's been hanging out by this brook during a time of drought, and I'm sure that over time the formerly gushing brook gradually slowed to a trickle before drying up completely. So Elijah had to see this coming.

My guess is that he's sitting there and he's watching and he's thinking, "The water's not moving as fast as it used to... Guess the Lord is getting ready to do something..."

And as the water slowed a bit more, "You know, Lord, anytime now would be nice..." And the water's just trickling, "Hey, God, I'm still out here, You know... You got another plan for me?"

And then there's nothing!

"God?! Hello!?!?! You still there, God? I'm still HERE! Like YOU said! What now?" And it's like the Lord sort of leaves him hanging...

We don't know the time frame between verse 7 and verse 8, but what we know is that eventually - sometime AFTER the brook dried up - *Then the Lord said to Elijah, "Go...."* (1 Kings 17:8a).

God was not surprised that the brook had dried up.

He had seen it coming. He could have prevented it from drying up, but He didn't. He was getting ready to do something new in Elijah's life. God was preparing a new place of ministry for Elijah, and He was preparing Elijah for a new place of ministry.

God had not forgotten Elijah or Elijah's need.

Is the brook drying up where you are today?

Has it already dried up? I want you (and me!) to be encouraged today - God is not going to stop providing for you. It may look that way at the moment, but the nature of God does not change. He is good and He is loving, and He always has your best interest at heart.

So while you are waiting by the drying brook, be encouraged - it just may be that God is preparing to do something new in your life.

Wait for His provision, and I suspect you will find - as Elijah did - that God will supply (in HIS time and in HIS way) all that you need.

ORDER OF
OPERATIONS

Yes, he humbled you by letting you go hungry and then feeding you with manna, a food previously unknown to you and your ancestors. He did it to teach you that people do not live by bread alone; rather we live by every word that comes from the mouth of the Lord.
Deuteronomy 8:3 NLT

When I was learning math, I remember having to learn an "order of operations". Problems had to be worked out in the right order, or else I would get a wrong answer.

What I've come to realize is that the same thing is true in life - there is an order of operations.

For things to work out right, I have to be sure to put things in the right order. Often, it's a matter or prioritizing correctly. Sometimes, though, it's just about practicality and common sense - like if I try to put the cups in my kitchen cabinet before the coffee mugs, the mugs don't fit and I end up having to take the cups back out. I know this "order of operations" because I experienced some aggravation in trying to figure out how things fit together when space is limited.

In speaking of how the Lord sent manna to the children of Israel, we find that there was an "order of operations" at work here.

The Scripture says, *"he humbled you by letting you go hungry **and then** feeding you with manna...".*

AND THEN!
The Lord could have sent manna from day 1. It wouldn't have been a hard thing for Him to do. He had the power. He knew that the people would need to eat.   But He also knew that there was something that they needed more than food, only they didn't realize it yet.

They needed HIM!

Food was incidental, but the people didn't know it. So God let them go hungry. Not for long - He didn't take them to the brink of starvation or anything close to it. But He let them go hungry, and after they had been hungry for a little while, God sent the manna.

When we've waited for the manna, our faith grows - like the Children of Israel. We learn that what matters most may not necessarily be what we thought was most important. But we learn.

God provides.

It's generally not in the way we expect. It's often not as quickly as we really want. But God provides.

Are you hungry today? Are you in need of something? Rest assured God knows what you need. He is not insensitive to your needs. Probably He is just stretching you to grow your faith - helping you to understand that "man does not live by bread alone."

Hang in there. Manna's coming!

THROUGH THE DEEP

When you go through the deep waters, I will be with you.
When you go through rivers of difficulty, you will not
drown. When you walk through the fire of oppression, you
will not be burned up; the flames will not consume you.
Isaiah 43:2 NLT

Often when we talk about our trusting in the Lord, we present our faith as based on His blessing us and helping us through difficult times. This line of thought can leave us with a distorted view of God and salvation.
God is holy, and cannot tolerate sin. If we want to be with God, we have to deal with our sin problem. Jesus Christ offered His life as payment for our sins.

This is the basis of our salvation.

Now, for the rest of the story.

Along with salvation, the Lord has offered us some "fringe benefits". These benefits are based on God's goodness - not our worthiness. Sometimes, these benefits are misrepresented.

I often hear well-meaning people (and I have been guilty of this as well) talk about how God has changed their life and given them peace, joy, deliverance, what ever... While peace, joy, deliverance, and all those other blessings are wonderful gifts from God, they are just fringe benefits of our relationship with God.

In other words, if I come to God just for what He's going to do for me, I will find myself feeling let down, disillusioned, maybe even unloved.

I think this may be much of what has happened in modern Christianity - in focusing on the benefits, we have lost sight of the relationship, and the reason we truly need a Savior. People who came to Christ looking for a better life have run into the harsh realities of life. Life is hard. It's often not fair. The good guys don't always win. And being a Christian doesn't mean things will always go right for you. What it really means is that while things are going wrong, you're not alone.

Notice what Isaiah says, "**WHEN you go through deep waters...** (emphasis mine)."

This is not the feel good message of, "Don't worry - God will get you out of the deep waters."

The promise is that when we find ourselves in deep waters (and we WILL find ourselves in deep waters), God will be with us. He *might* deliver us - and sometimes He does and it's wonderful. But ALWAYS He will be with us.

Do you find yourself in deep waters today? If you know the Lord, then you can rest in the knowledge that you are not alone.

GO WITH WHAT
YOU KNOW

The human heart is the most deceitful of all things, and desperately wicked. Who really knows how bad it is?
Jeremiah 17:9 NLT

"Go with what you know." This is what the Lord has been teaching me lately. Interestingly, it is a principle that has applied in every situation in which I have been called on for counsel lately. Go with what you know...
It's very simple, really, and yet my failure to fully understand this principle seems to be at the heart of every struggle, and certainly at the heart of every worry.

The problem is this: I am human. Not only that, I am a woman! I am prone to emotion, often letting my emotions get the best of me, being carried away by my feelings...!

So here is the thing I am learning - my feelings will carry me far away from the truth if I do not carefully guard my heart and walk confidently in the faith which I profess.

This should not be surprising. The Bible tells us it will happen: "the heart is deceitful...". Just feeling something "in my heart" doesn't make it right. In fact, I think that may be the root of most sin: following the heart. We use that phrase, "just following my heart," to justify every irresponsible behavior, from men and women who leave their spouses, to parents who neglect their children so they can follow their own dreams.

This "go with what you know" principle, I'm finding, is really the key to daily living. On a most basic level, it is the key to eating more healthy: I may *feel* like single-handedly downing a dozen KrispyKremes, but if I "go with what I know," I can save myself the misery that follows the dozen doughnuts AND the months of exercise it will take to counteract them!

On a spiritual level, it's the key to experiencing God's peace in my life. If I go with my feelings, my days will be plagued by things like worry, laziness, self-indulgence, and anxiety. But if I will simply "go with what I know," what I know is that the God I serve is powerful, and His grace is sufficient.

So let me encourage you today: Go with what you know!

THE TRUTH IN TRIALS

While Jesus was in the Temple, he watched the rich
people dropping their gifts in the collection box.
Then a poor widow came by and dropped in two small
coins. "I tell you the truth," Jesus said, "this poor
widow has given more than all the rest of them. For
they have given a tiny part of their surplus, but she,
poor as she is, has given everything she has."
Luke 21:1-4 NLT

I have often wondered how modern "name it and claim it" preachers interpret this story...

Our modern view of Christianity is that Jesus came to give us a better life, yet here we have a very clear picture of a faithful follower of the Lord who was not enjoying the "benefits" of her faith.

This presents us with an interesting dilemma. Either this woman had a faith problem that had left her in poverty, or we have a poor understanding of what Christ came to the earth to do.

Some modern teachers would have to suggest that this woman had an obvious lack of faith, evidenced by the fact that she was utterly destitute. Perhaps some sin in her life, or faithlessness left her in financial bondage when Jesus Christ had come to set her free...

This explanation doesn't work, because it undermines the Lord's commendation of the woman's actions. Why would Jesus commend the faith of the faithless? He would NOT. So there must be another explanation...

Could it be that modern Christianity has distorted the Gospel to the point that we no longer understand why Christ came?

Jesus Christ did not come so that this widow could enjoy health, wealth, and a good life on earth. What He came to do for this widow was not to bless her finances. He didn't come to rescue her from financial troubles. He came because this woman - and you and I - had a sin problem. What we need is not financial blessing. What we need is salvation!

Jesus Christ came because "the wages of sin is death" and without His willingness to pay the price for our sins, we are utterly doomed.

So does this mean that Christ wasn't concerned with the widow's financial situation? Not at all.

We don't know what happened to the widow after she had given her last pennies in offering to the Lord. Did she starve to death because she had no money left to buy food? Did she lose her home because she had no means to pay her bills? Did Jesus miraculously provide for her, blessing her beyond measure?

Or just maybe, did one of Jesus listeners that day hear the truth of the woman's plight and recognize an opportunity to live out the faith about which Christ was teaching?

HALLELUJAH!

One day some parents brought their children to Jesus so he could touch and bless them. But the disciples scolded the parents for bothering him. When Jesus saw what was happening, he was angry with his disciples. He said to them, "Let the children come to me. Don't stop them! For the Kingdom of God belongs to those who are like these children.
Mark 10:13-14 NLT

A few years ago at a kids camp where we were ministering, the band had just finished playing. The final song had a "Hallelujah" in it. Seizing the moment, the chapel speaker for the week began to ask the children about the song.

"Does anybody know what 'hallelujah' means?" the speaker asked.

Without hesitation one little girl piped up and said, "Yay!"

The speaker took this answer as a good beginning and began to explain the component of the word 'hallelujah' that indicated the name of God, at which point the children concluded that 'hallelu-jah' means, "Yay, God!"

I don't know if that definition would really satisfy the seminary professors, but I was touched by the truth and simplicity of the children's understanding. We adults really have a knack for complicating things, don't we?

The next day I was back in chapel, scoping things out in what I like to call my "mean mom" mode - giving kids "the eye" for distracting the others around them. A pair of boys caught my eye sitting by themselves while the others were down in front singing and worshipping. These two boys were deeply involved in something that was definitely not the song being sung up front. They were laughing and poking each other, so I wandered over to check things out. What I found brought a smile to my face, and fresh hope to my heart. One of the boys had his Bible open, and he was pointing things out to the other boy. It was one of those kids' Bibles with nice color pictures interspersed through the pages. Probably they were laughing at a picture that they thought was silly, but that didn't really matter. One would turn the page and point out something else, and they would both laugh. Then the other would grab the Bible and flip some pages, and find something to show the first boy. These boys may have had no idea what song the others were singing. I'm sure they had little understanding of the significance of the words they were reading or the pictures they were laughing at. But whatever their motivation, these boys had an enjoyable encounter with God's Word that evening. And if all they got from it is that there's some funny stuff in the Bible, it's a start. Maybe it will be enough to bring them back looking for more...

And I began to wonder, do I still have any "shock and awe" as I read the Bible? Or, have I gotten so 'mature' that I cannot appreciate the awesomeness of my God and His Word like these little children were doing?

So I just want to take a minute today and say, "Yay God!"

BUILDING BRIDGES

*There is salvation in no one else! God has given no
other name under heaven by which we must be saved.*
Acts 4:12 NLT

As we've been driving cross country lately (we left Maine last Monday and are currently in Texas headed for New Mexico), I've been noticing a lot of road construction. That in itself is not unusual - annoying, but not unusual. What IS interesting is that in almost every state, much of the road construction has centered around building bridges - or rather, REbuilding bridges.

In just the little bit of news I've managed to keep up with over the past few years, I remember specifically two major incidents involving highway bridges collapsing, resulting in multiple fatalities and injuries. So I thought that might explain the attention to the bridges I've observed of late. I don't know if the repairs were legislated or voluntary, but I think it's a great idea - and not just because I cross so many of them on a regular basis.

A faulty bridge is dangerous. It is closely akin to walking on thin ice. By the time you realize there is a problem, it is generally too late to avoid serious consequences.

In our world today, many are traveling on faulty bridges that they think will lead to life. The problem is, unless someone who sees they are in danger warns them, only death awaits. Whether it is fame, power, achievement, money, good works, religion, or some other "bridge", all of these methods are shaky in the beginning, and ultimately all will collapse.

There is only one way to heaven, only one bridge that will not collapse: saving faith in Jesus Christ based on His sacrifice on the cross. Only genuine repentance - that not only acknowledges "I'm on the wrong bridge," but that also turns around, gets off the wrong path and on the right one - produces genuine faith.

And only genuine faith leads to salvation.

Is the bridge you're on safe? Don't take chances. Your life depends on it - forever!

THE IRONY OF IT ALL...

"For I know the plans I have for you," declares the Lord, "plans to prosper you and not to harm you, plans to give you hope and a future."
Jeremiah 29:11 NIV.

I was thinking today how very much out of my comfort zone much of my life is has been. And I was also struck by the fact that most of the people who have seen me over the years might not really see the irony in the things that I have done. For years, I engaged with my family in full-time, very public ministry.

Our inside joke is that I don't really like people! At least, that's what I say.

That statement is not entirely true; however, it does bring home the point that left to myself, I could happily live on a deserted island. I would gladly take the back seat in life, stay out of the limelight, and reshelve books in a library somewhere.

By nature, I am NOT a social person. Personal interaction is hard work for me, so I avoid it whenever possible. Even though at times I have been called upon to speak to groups of students, children, and even adults - sometimes large groups - if you put me in a room where I have to relate to people on a more personal level, and I panic! Not noticeably, I hope, but definitely, inside, I just would prefer to go hide in a back corner somewhere and sneak out after everybody else is gone.

I don't do that - usually - because in spite of the joke that I don't like people, the truth is that I have this LOVE for people that compels me to step out of what is comfortable. And really, more than a love for people is a love for the Savior who stepped far out of His comfort zone for me.

A few years ago, I was at a church that did what they called a "spiritual gift inventory". I was very disappointed in the process because basically all that was accomplished is that people took a little test that confirmed what they LIKE to do. And while I certainly think that if you can do something for the Lord that you like, you should by all means do it, I don't think that the Lord necessarily chooses to use us most effectively while we are *just* doing the things we like. I think that His purposes often involve stretching us beyond what we can do comfortably on our own. Now that is not to say that the Lord wants us to be miserable. But He does call us to be faithful.

He puts us in positions to do things that we cannot do without Him.

I am reminded of the apostle Peter who encountered Jesus one day while he was well within his comfort zone: the fisherman was in the boat (see Matthew 14). It didn't really take a lot of faith for Peter to stay in the boat- that's something he had experience at. But stepping out of the boat - now that's a different story! The scary thing about walking on water, Peter discovered, was that you can't do it on your own. The ONLY way to do it is by keeping your eyes on Jesus, walking literally by faith and not by sight.

So when God said through Jeremiah *"I know the plans I have..."*, He was referring to plans that would be different from our own - plans that might be uncomfortable or scary or completely out of character. That was the case with the captives to whom this verse was written, and that will be the case with you and I as well.

So before you go getting too comfortable with your plans, better see what the Lord has in mind.

It probably won't be easy, and it may not be anything you ever pictured yourself doing, but hold on tight - it will be an amazing journey!

THE DESIRES OF
YOUR HEART

Delight yourself in the LORD, and He will
give you the desires of your heart.
Psalm 37:4 ESV

I t seems that the Lord often chooses to use us while we are doing things we may not necessarily "like" on our own. That is not to say that God wants to make us miserable, or that His plan for us is going to be something that we will be unhappy doing. Quite the opposite is true.

What often happens is that God chooses to move us out of our comfort zone into a place where we must rely more fully on Him. As Christians, we are fond of talking about the faith that we have, and we sing about how we are "desperate for Him" and "lost without Him". But the actual working of faith in our lives is often very different from the faith that we profess.

It is "out of our comfort zone" where we come to understand that God is far less concerned with our comfort than with our holiness. It is in those uncomfortable places that we discover if we are going to follow Him only when it's convenient and when He's letting us do things our own way, or if we really do trust Him with our lives.

But, you say, "Doesn't the Bible say that God will give us the desires of our hearts?"

Absolutely. I think, though, that when we look at that promise as a sort of "blank check" from God, we completely misinterpret what He is saying. If God actually gave me everything my heart desires, it would go against the very nature of God. He is GOOD. And what I have found, and what Scripture confirms, is that my heart is deceitful – it will mislead me.

So what I find in this promise of God to give me the desires of my heart is not that He is offering me a blank check of self-indulgence. Rather, what happens is *He gives me the desires of my heart* – in other words, when I am walking closely with Him, I desire what He desires.

In real life, what that means is that I can do things I never thought I would be able to do. I can enjoy things that I could never even attempt in my own strength. I can even 'like' things that would otherwise strike great fear and trembling in my heart. (And truthfully, sometimes there is still a little fear and trembling – that's just the enemy trying to rob me of a blessing. Fortunately, the love of God casts out fear, so trusting in Him moves me past the fear.)

So rest assured that God's plan for you is not to make you miserable and to force you to do something that you don't want to do. He may just want to broaden your horizons and introduce you to opportunities you never thought possible!

ABOUT THE AUTHOR

Susan T. Becker

 Writing in various formats since childhood, Susan T. Becker has been blogging as "The Invisible Woman" since 2009. From 2000-2012, Susan traveled in itinerant ministry with her family as Jeremiah 29:11 Ministries. Married to Jeff Becker since 1991, Susan is mother to two amazing young adults and grammy to the sweetest little guy on the planet.

Susan and Jeff currently reside in Dunnellon, Florida, where they serve as houseparents to children in the foster care system.

Find more from Susan at www.susantbecker.com.

Made in the USA
Columbia, SC
04 January 2025

48900234R00093